THE WOMEN'S MOVEMENT
IN THE CHURCH OF ENGLAND: 1850–1930

The Women's Movement in the Church of England 1850–1930

BRIAN HEENEY

Clarendon Press · Oxford
1988

Oxford University Press, Walton Street, Oxford OX2 6DP
Oxford New York Toronto
Delhi Bombay Calcutta Madras Karachi
Petaling Jaya· Singapore Hong Kong Tokyo
Nairobi Dar es Salaam Cape Town
Melbourne Auckland
and associated companies in
Beirut Berlin Ibadan Nicosia

Oxford is a trade mark of Oxford University Press

Published in the United States
by Oxford University Press, New York

British Library Cataloguing in Publication Data
Heeney, Brian
The women's movement in the Church of
England: 1850–1930.
1. Women in the Church of England—History
I. Title
262'.15   BX5182.3
ISBN 0-19-822671-3

Library of Congress Cataloging in Publication Data
Heeney, Brian, 1933–1983.
The women's movement in the Church of England, 1850–1930/Brian
Heeney.
Includes index.
1. Women in the Anglican Communion—England—History—19th
century.   2. Women in the Anglican Communion—England—History—20th
century.   3. Feminism—Religious aspects—Church of England—History of
doctrines—19th century.   4. Feminism—Religious aspects—Church of England—
History of doctrines—20th century.   5. Church of England— Doctrines—History—
19th century.   6. Church of England— Doctrines— History— 20th century.
7. Anglican Communion— Doctrines— History— 19th century.   8. Anglican
Communion—Doctrines—History—20th century.   9. Church of England—
History—19th century.   10. Church of England— History—20th century.
11. Anglican Communion—England—History—19th century. 12. Anglican
Communion—England—History—20th century. 13. England—Church history—19th
century.   14. England—Church history—20th century.   I. Title.
BX5182.3.H43 1988   283'.42'088042—dc19   87-29804
ISBN 0-19-822671-3

Set by Downdell Ltd
Printed in Great Britain
at the University Printing House, Oxford
by David Stanford
Printer to the University

TO GOODITH FEILDING HEENEY
with love and affection

Brian Heeney, 1933–1983

THE manuscript of this book was left by the author when he died, aged 49, on 17 September 1983. After deliberation, three of his friends decided to prepare it for the press. They are conscious that parts of the book were prepared in a race against mortality. They decided to amend the text only when stylistic felicity or accuracy seemed to demand it.

In presenting Brian Heeney's manuscript for publication, they had two main considerations in mind. First, here was a study which, if lacking its final polish, nevertheless helped to open up a subject of importance both for women's studies in general and for the debate concerning the role of women in the ministry of the Church, to which it can offer some historical perspective. In some respects the debate has moved on a long way since Louise Creighton or Maude Royden, but the arguments put forward on either side, as well as the strong emotions which they rationalize, are still evident today.

The second reason for publishing this small book is to commemorate a talent and a personality cut tragically short. Brian Heeney made an unusual impact on those who knew him. Though the son of one of Canada's leading diplomats, Arnold Heeney, and reared as a young man in the embassy world of Ottawa, Paris, and Washington, he did not choose a career in government service, to which he would have been well suited, but elected to follow his paternal grandfather and seek ordination in the Anglican Church. He studied history at Trinity College in the University of Toronto and trained as a priest at the General Theological Seminary in New York and at the Episcopal Theological School in Cambridge, Massachusetts, where he took a BD. Then, on the avuncular advice of his father's old tutor, W. C. Costin, President of St John's College, Oxford, always on the lookout for talented and personable

North Americans, he was induced to enrol as a graduate student in Oxford. There he wrote a D.Phil. thesis, on the Woodard Schools, later published as his first book, *Mission to the Middle Classes*. From 1964 to 1971 he taught history at the University of Alberta, where he was Anglican chaplain. Thereafter he moved to Trent University where he com- bined the teaching of history with a number of administrative posts—master of Champlain College, director of the Bata Library, and finally academic vice-president and provost.

In our age of career specialization it is not very usual to find a man combining simultaneous careers as priest, administrator, and scholar, though this would seem rather less surprising among North American clergy today or in the Victorian world of clerical headmasters and academics of which Brian Heeney wrote. Had he pursued any one avocation exclusively, he would probably have risen sooner to high office: had he lived longer he could have become a bishop or a college president and he would certainly have written more books. Instead, he choose to integrate all three careers in a way that seemed so entirely natural that it did not arouse comment or even reflection among his friends. He himself clearly thought about it, however, and his writing on the pastoral ministry suggests that he had a well-considered position which came near to that of the mid-Victorian pastors he most admired—men like Harry Jones, Broad churchman, slum priest and civic improver, and friend of F. D. Maurice, who did not accept the notion of clerical apartness, and for whom (in Brian Heeney's own words) 'the distinction between secular and sacred was unreal, and who viewed all work for the good of man as properly pastoral'. For Heeney, teaching, the writing of history, the running of a college or a library, was a religious vocation, to be undertaken naturally and without fuss. Like Harry Jones, however, he did not see the pastor as a man to be judged by his works alone. He accepted and lived up to the ideal set up for the Victorian priest by the clerical writers whom he described in *A Different Kind of Gentleman*; the pastor was a man whose ministry 'was at least as much in his being as in his doing, in his character as in his activity'.

Activity he certainly showed. He had a large endowment of that North American energy which awes and occasionally alarms the British. He worked extremely hard and played hard too; as a colleague noted, 'he would swim, play tennis or squash, and sail with the energy of a little boy who had to do it or explode'. He was a meticulous forward-planner and gained great satisfaction from organizing the future—plotting the outline of his next book and arranging his next study leave in Oxford almost before the present one had ended. Remarkably, however, he combined his activism with patience and flexibility of mind: though his best laid plans went 'oft agley', he did not recriminate or fret or fume but started optimistically on another plan. Organizational disasters such as the famous family holiday in Ireland—home of the Heeneys—where the landlady fed whiskey to the baby, the bedroom chamber pots were already full on arrival, and the ceiling, with a tank full of water, fell on Brian while he was in the bath—rapidly became the stuff of delighted anecdote. Though massively endowed with common sense, he was no Benthamite; he had an uproarious sense of humour and an amused fascination with the bizarre, which was one of the reasons for his enjoyment of Oxford, with its rich complement of eccentrics, lay and clerical. He relished the more exotic items tucked away in the columns of the *Church Times*; he was fascinated by the academically-dressed gentleman to be found in Broad Street gazing intently through the slots of letter boxes. He enjoyed the diversity of English life and the way in which the Church of England reflected it.

He was not a high sacerdotalist, not a metaphysician or a mystic but a man very much in this world. At the same time he accepted wholeheartedly the central importance of the sacramental life of the church to which he belonged and the principle of Apostolicity on which it rested. But he gave plenty of space to natural religion. To him religion seemed to come naturally. It began in his family with grace at meals and spread outwards to the extended family of the Church and world. It came easily to him as master of Champlain College to hold services in his living room for those who wished to come. In his summers at the Lac des

Isles in the Laurentians, where the Heeneys had a cabin, surrounded by a scattered colony of relations and friends, neighbouring families converged by canoe, car, and foot to services at which he would preach, informally and unself-consciously, in open-necked shirt, slacks, and sandals.

Mark Pattison observed of Victorian Oxford how its leading men of thirty-five or forty were struck by an intellectual palsy and betook themselves not to port, but to the work of attending boards and negotiating some phantom of legislation with all the importance of a cabinet council. They gave to the university the 'tone of a lively municipal borough; all the objects of science and learning for which a university exists being put out of sight by the consideration of the material means of endowing them'. This could not be said of Brian Heeney. He was an out-standing administrator, working with efficiency, ration-ality, humanity, and celerity—it was observed of him that no piece of paper passed over his desk twice. Like so many good university administrators, however, he suc-ceeded because his heart was not totally in his task; he was not committed to bureaucracy as an end in itself. No matter how hard-pressed, he insisted on giving priority to his teaching, which he refused to abandon, and he was always, at some mental level, brooding on his next book. His family observed that at moments of maximum tension he would take out his reader's card for the Bodleian Library and look at it. This element ¯of scholarly detachment from administrative problems was useful, for problems were not lacking: he was master of a college during a period of student unrest and provost at a time when universities had to face unpalatable cuts. He had a reputation for the utmost fairness: when communicating or making unpleasant decisions he never fudged but explained carefully the rational grounds for the action. He was trusted. He was what he appeared to be, and every-one knew it.

In writing history he showed the same qualities. He did not spread his wings in high imaginative flights, nor did he try to penetrate into the deeper recesses of human moti-vation, but he was always shrewd, fair-minded, and clear.

The choice of Victorian religion for his speciality was a sensible one, for he brought to bear on it both the detachment of a Canadian and the inside knowledge of an Anglican priest and pastor. By the time he died he was getting nicely into his stride. His study of Victorian pastoral theory, *A Different Kind of Gentleman*, won a prize and is an important work for all who study nineteenth-century religion. For some time he had been accumulating materials on women's work in the Victorian Church. This interest had been set in motion once he realized the extent to which women—be they parson's wives and daughters, Sunday School teachers, district visitors, Ranyard biblewomen, or nuns—were essential to the success of Victorian Anglicanism, yet had been relegated to the margins in its synods and counsels. Moreover, they had been woefully, perhaps wilfully, ignored by those who wrote its history. A determination, almost a passion, to put the record straight carried him through his final years of sickness and pain. This book is the product of those last years. It falls short of its author's intentions. But we offer it both as a contribution to church history in its own right and as an act of remembrance of a good man.

Contents

Introduction

THIS book describes the growth of early Church feminism in England, a twentieth-century rebellion against the tradition of Victorian women's subordination to men. At first the context of subordination was overwhelming, suffocating the new voices raised against its pressures. In the late nineteenth-century the Church of England provided a good deal of anti-feminist doctrine and was a major centre of resistance to the women's movement generally. None the less, the institution was becoming feminized as women's place became larger and larger in Church life; biblical criticism made possible a liberal interpretation of those parts of scripture upon which Church 'antis' built their arguments, and assertive churchwomen developed a self-conciousness based on increasing education and participation in the community generally. Church feminism became evident in the 1890s, first mixed with the movement for democratic church-manship, an effort by women to share in Church councils. It was also apparent in a reinterpretation of the ideology of domesticity and the traditional understanding of the relationship of the sexes. Church feminists sought a reasonable share (different women interpreted 'reasonable' differently) in Church government, in lay leadership of public worship, and in the charter role of the Church's professional ministry (pastoral, homiletic, liturgical).

Church feminism grew within a very traditional and tradition-bound body. At one extreme it inspired radical demands and attracted a few churchwomen who were actively involved in non-ecclesiastical feminist movements, notably that for the parliamentary suffrage. At the other extreme it provoked violent reaction, fervent expression of commitment to women's subordination, and firm determination to keep women from places of ecclesiastical power and authority. Many were those whose response was calmer, who were willing to modify traditional attitudes, biblical interpretations, and church practices, but who were unprepared for revolutionary change (such as opening the priesthood to women). The actions and arguments of Church feminists and their opponents were the outward and visible signs of changing attitudes and conflicting views within the Church about women's place in society, secular as well as ecclesiastical.

By 1930 Church feminism had achieved a measure of success, although it was far short of achieving equal status and professional opportunity for women in the Church; nor had it converted the Church of England to a feminist theology. After 1930 the movement stalled, not to be reactivated until the 1970s.

PART I.

The Context of Subordination

1

Woman's Image and Place in the Victorian Church

THE Church of England in the late nineteenth century was a significant national body to which a substantial (although declining) number of Englishmen and women claimed allegiance, and in which the proportion of active membership seems to have been increasingly female. Anxiety about the high proportion of women at religious services was evident from about 1880. It was intensified by Charles Booth's discovery that, in London, 'the female sex forms the mainstay of every religious assembly of whatever class', and by the statistics in Richard Mudie-Smith's survey of *The Religious Life of London* at the beginning of the new century which showed that nearly twice as many women attended Church of England services as men. It was a trend which the First World War evidently accelerated.[1] Thus the feminist movement appeared at a time when men seemed, in terms of numbers, on the defensive within the Church.

Furthermore, churchwomen did not simply sing, pray, and listen in church. Looking back over seventy years in 1919, a committee appointed by the archbishop of Canterbury to study the ministry of women attributed much of 'the immense expansion of activity and of efficiency in ministry to the religious needs of the people' to 'the wonderful work accomplished by the mainly voluntary efforts of women'. Voluntary effort was supplemented by the labour of paid workers of various types and by the growing number of women committed to the religious life. The archbishop's committee wondered at the 'extraordinary

[1] Owen Chadwick, *The Victorian Church* (London, 1970), ii. 222; Charles Booth, *Life and Labour of the People in London*, third series: *Religious Influences* (London, 1902), vii. 424; Richard Mudie-Smith (ed.), *The Religious Life of London* (London, 1904), 267, 267, 443. See also *Manchester Guardian*, 12 June 1915.

amount of good work . . . achieved by women' since
1850 'under the different heads of district visiting,
Sunday-School teaching, Church music, parochial clubs,
missionary societies, study circles, rescue and preventative
agencies, besides the larger organizations represented by
the Sisterhoods and Deaconess Institutions, by the Girls'
Friendly Society and the Mothers' Union.' Added to all
these were the accomplishments of 'hundreds . . . of
wives, widows and daughters of clergymen, and of single
women, who in obscurity have dedicated their lives and
their substance to the promotion of the Kingdom of God in
our own country and in heathen lands'.[2]

Although women were playing such a substantial role in
the Church, it was a body in which the women's movement had some difficulty taking hold. The institution was
widely seen, and many of its leaders confirmed the view,
as a guardian of basic anti-feminist doctrine rooted in the
Pentateuch and enshrined in the Pauline epistles. It was
easy for Christians, speaking and preaching to largely
uncritical or traditionalist congregations, to define as
God's law both the notion of woman's subordination to
man and also the propriety of her prime concern with
home and family. On the whole, church people accepted
what they heard in the pulpit, especially if the preacher
wore purple.

The women's movement in the Church, as elsewhere,
was fundamentally a movement which rejected the
doctrine of female subordination, a doctrine which, the
movement's exponents believed, had frequently trapped
women into narrow roles and often enfeebled their lives.
The women's movement was against belief in women's
subordination to a male ruling class, against automatic
submission to husband, father, or brother. This opposition
took many forms as women in different situations sought
to break out of the protective and confining boxes into
which the tradition of submission had placed them in
home and Church.

---

[2] *The Ministry of Women: A Report by a Committee Appointed by His Grace the Lord Archbishop of Canterbury* (London, 1919), 22.

Among church people the doctrine of submission assumed a theological, indeed a biblical form, for it had been cast in this form by leaders who relentlessly hammered home the 'obvious' lesson of Genesis and St Paul. The creation myth in Genesis, according to which woman was created from man, after man, and for man's advantage, together with the regrettable incidents that follow, were the biblical foundations of subordination. Thus one finds the 'divine law' that 'man should be head of the woman' clearly based on Genesis 3: 16.[3] J. W. Burgon, a prominent High Churchman, based his opposition for modern education for women on the same ground: he pointed out in 1884 that the 'reason for Women's creation [is] distinctly assigned. She is intended to be Man's "help"—Man's *helper* . . . a second self. Yet not a rival self.' He went on, 'St. Paul's teaching concerning Woman is built entirely on the narrative in Genesis: thus proving that the primaeval decree concerning her is a thing for all time'. In the very same year in which Burgon put forward his cautions about women, Bishop Christopher Wordsworth of Lincoln, father of the founder of Lady Margaret Hall at Oxford and a cautious supporter of his daughter's cause, laid down a remarkably succinct and clear statement of the doctrine of subordination in a sermon on 'Christian Womanhood'. Building largely on the supposed historicity of Genesis 2, he concluded that 'her [woman's] existence was not only subsequent to that of man, but was derived from it. She was after man, out of man and for man.' He went on to develop the theme (very common among churchmen and conservative-minded educators) that 'anything that disturbs that subordination weakens her authority and mars her dignity and beauty. Her true strength is in loyal submission.' A few years earlier Charlotte Yonge in *Womankind* had affirmed her 'full belief in the inferiority of women' and did so on the basis of the old story that 'when the test came whether the two human beings would pay allegiance to God or to the Tempter, it was the woman who was first to fall, and to draw her husband into the

---

[3] See e.g. 'The Social Position of Women', *Churchman's Magazine*, Oct. 1857.

same transgression. Hence her punishment of physical weakness and subordination.' The same sort of thing lay behind the argument of Miss E. J. Whately (in a paper at the 1878 Church Congress read for her by a man) that women *did* have a role in church work; for 'as woman was appointed the helpmate of man in . . . [the family], so she is in . . . [the Church]'.[4]

Such firm conviction of woman's subordination was based on the Old Testament. It was apparently supported and confirmed by certain remarks of St Paul in the New Testament. To the Corinthians (1 Cor. 14: 34–5) he wrote, 'Women should not address the meeting. They have no licence to speak, but should keep their place as the law directs. If there is something they want to know, they can ask their own husbands at home. It is a shocking thing that a woman should address the congregation.' In the same letter, Chapter 11, Paul went on at length about the relative status of male and female, clearly deriving his view from the Genesis myth, as well as from contemporary culture. Thus 'while every man has Christ for his Head, woman's head is man' and 'man is the image of God, the mirror of his glory, whereas woman reflects the glory of man. For man did not originally spring from woman, but woman was made out of man; and man was not created for woman's sake, but woman for the sake of man.' The author of the first letter to Timothy (supposed to have been St Paul) enjoined 'a woman must be a learner, listening quietly and with due submission. I do not permit a woman to be a teacher, nor must woman domineer over man; she should be quiet.' He noted, by way of justification for the statement, that 'it was not Adam who was deceived; it was the woman who, yielding to deception, fell into sin' (1 Tim. 2: 11–14). Bishop Wordsworth based himself on such texts when he lashed out, in 1884, against those 'who flatter woman with specious words and tempt her to claim for herself an independent position and one in all respects

4 J. W. Burgon, *To Educate Young Women Like Young Men, and with Young Men; A Thing Inexpedient and Immodest* (London, 1884), 15–16; Christopher Wordsworth, *Christian Womanhood and Christian Sovereignty* (London, 1884), 10, 21; Charlotte M. Yonge, *Womankind* (London, 1876), 1; Church Congress Report (hereafter cited as CCR) (1878), 347.

of equality to that of Man'. Such agitations 'disturb her divinely-constituted relationship to man and to God, and despoil her of her true dignity and most attractive grace'.[5] As James Gibson wrote in 1894, 'from 'Moses to Paul is a wide jump, but Paul confirmed the subjection of women'.[6] It was a major task of the church feminists to re-interpret such texts as well as to stress other scriptural passages with meanings and implications supporting women's equality. However, until well into the twentieth century the advocates of subordination dominated the ecclesiastical scene.

There was one significant area of life in which the subordinate being was expected to take the initiative: the sphere of home and family. For this purpose women were held to be marvellously and delicately equipped by God and nature. There was no doubt in the minds of many conservative churchmen that widening a woman's horizons by introducing her into spheres hitherto reserved for men would weaken her natural domesticity, thereby threatening home and family life in general. Over and over again, home was brought forward as 'woman's appointed sphere'. J. W. Burgon noted that 'it is . . . in the sweet sanctities of domestic life—in home duties . . . that woman is taught by the Spirit to find scope for her activity . . . in a word *Home* is woman's place'. He dreaded the apparent urge of many modern women to abandon the world of the home for the public sphere and the professions: 'woman will too late discover that she has, as far as in her lay, unsexed herself; lost her present unique social position, come to be regarded only as an inferior kind of Man'. Sarah Austin, author of *Two Letters on Girls' Schools and on the Training of Working Women*, writing in 1857, affirmed that there was 'nothing higher than . . . the comfort, order and good government of the house and the instruction of the young', and Charlotte Yonge, in 1876, insisted that 'home-making is perhaps the most essential feature of all duties of womankind'. In the last quarter of the century speakers at Church congresses, a succession of bishops, laymen and

---

5 Wordsworth, *Christian Womanhood*, p. 25.
6 J. Gibson, *The Emancipation of Women*, 2nd edn. (London, 1894), 57.

women pressed the point, and the example of Christ's youthful home was brought forward as a model: 'what a home that must have been at Nazareth, where the Lord was brought up with Joseph and Mary; what a pure, blessed, peaceful, loving, home'. 'Ah dear sisters,' the bishop of Bedford exhorted an audience of working women in 1887, 'make your homes like those [sic] . . . where your husbands can love to come and sit.'[7]

Women were held responsible for domestic life, but even the most ardent enthusiast for that vocation did not attempt to keep them absolutely to their own hearth and home. Although Canon John Jebb of Hereford firmly asserted that 'in Church they [women] should appear strictly as members of families', he did not suggest they should be confined always to their own family groups: the domestic virtues were not much evident among the poor and deprived, so sadly remote from direct Church influence. What better way could ladies serve God than by extending the Christian ideals of home and family from their own to other people's domiciles, especially by participating in the widespread custom of 'district visiting'.[8]

Authors of mid-Victorian handbooks of pastoral theology, 'helps' to parish priests, emphasized the appropriate use of leisured ladies as aids to incumbents. J. H. Blunt, whose *Directorium Pastorale* was published in 1864, wrote a considerable section on the value of district visiting to the parish priest, to the poor, and to the ladies themselves who looked to it as 'relief from compulsory idleness or from occupations of a trivial character'. He was, however, extremely careful to warn the pastor to make sure that *primary* domestic obligations were fulfilled before parochial ones were undertaken and he made it clear who ought to be in control: 'parents have a *right* to be consulted, in every case, before their unmarried daughters are permitted to undertake . . . parochial visiting . . . The consent

    [7] J. W. Burgon, *Woman's Place: A Sermon* (Oxford and London, 1871), 6, 7, 10; Sarah Austin, *Two Letters on Girls' Schools and on the Training of Working Women* (London, 1857), 20; Yonge, *Womankind*, p. 264; CCR (1887), 449. See also CCR (1878), 341, 342; (1885), 160; (1891), 386; (1895), 498.
    [8] John Jebb, 'Three Lectures on the Cathedral Service of the Church of England', in *The Christians' Miscellany* (Leeds, 1841).

of husbands, in like cases, seems too much a matter of mere propriety to need urging.' A few years after Blunt wrote, the anonymous author of *Hints to District Visitors* made it very clear indeed that an important test for the prospective visitor was her own domestic record: 'the woman who has been most helpful in her own circle . . . will excel most when any higher mission calls forth her latest power'. One of the greatest advantages of this sort of external work for women was the opportunity it provided 'to combine active charity with domestic duty: she can be a sister of mercy abroad, while she still remains a dutiful daughter at home'. Furthermore, as we shall see below, the tradition of subordination to man was maintained, for all district visitors worked under the authority of the appropriate parish priest.[9] The domestic vocation, whether in its primary form (the woman's own home and family) or in an extended version (a mission to other families or individuals in need), was always what Bishop E. S. Talbot of Southwark called in 1910 'fostering work': 'its activities broaden out from the home and from woman's first duty; it is still the wifeliness and the motherliness which she has to carry out into the world'.[10]

Just as Victorian Anglican defenders of subordination found a powerful biblical base for their view of women, so the promoters of women's domestic vocation found a biblical heroine: Mary, the mother of Jesus. She was alleged to have raised the status of domesticity and to have 'ennobled, elevated, sanctified' woman's place in the 'design of the great Creator'. In 1881 E. W. Sargeant preached a sermon on 'Woman's Glory' which was really about the Virgin Mary and her special qualities of 'faith', 'constancy', and 'modesty'. The last signalled Mary's contentment 'to further and sustain the enterprise and courage of the Man. . . . Enough for her that she was the chosen vessel that held the world's true Light. There is not a hint that she thought herself or desired to be thought

---

[9] J. H. Blunt, *Directorium Pastorale: Principles and Practise of Pastoral Work in the Church of England* (London, 1864), 325, 328–9; *Hints to District Visitors* (London, 1858), 55, 15.

[10] CCR (1910), 322.

more than that implies.'[11] In the twentieth century Mary continued to be an anchor for the doctrine of domesticity and was used to demonstrate first, that this vocation was primary, available directly or indirectly to virtually all women, and second, that other vocations, especially within the Church, which were not shared or adumbrated by Mary, were inappropriate for Christian womanhood.

Mary's personal qualities, said Lady Acland in 1908, were those of the 'spiritual woman, pure, unselfish, patient, humble', entirely suitable to a life of due submission to the appropriate male and of devotion to the vital (though modest) domestic round. In 1921, by which time the traditional world of the churchman was being challenged on a number of fronts, one arch-conservative, Canon Sparrow Simpson, still clung to Mary's idolized and subordinate character:

What deeply impressed the primitive Christian world was the quiet unobtrusive place occupied by the Mother of God in the assemblies of the Apostolic Church. She was present, and that is all that can be said. She certainly never preached; still less did she celebrate the Eucharist. She must have thought that in this restraint she was acting in accordance with the mind of her Son.[12]

Over and over again Mary-like characteristics were defined as the highest female qualities. As early as 1838, the author of *Hints to a Clergyman's Wife* found the 'distinguishing characteristics of the female' to be 'tenderness and compassion' which the writer believed would greatly add to a clergyman's ministry. Charlotte Yonge wrote of 'efficiency, sympathy, cheerfulness, unselfishness and sweet-temper' and saw woman as 'viewing the utmost sacrifice of herself as simply natural'. In his recent book, *Woman and Philanthropy in Nineteenth-Century England*, Frank Prochaska has distilled the positive qualities of later Victorian female passivity with skill, emphasizing the

[11] Burgon, *Woman's Place*, p. 5; E. W. Sergeant, *Woman's Glory* (London, 1881), 14.

[12] *Pan-Anglican Papers . . . The Church and its Ministry: The Ministry of Women* (London, 1908), 25; CCR (1921), 227.

religious and moral qualities which were attributed to that portion of the human race.[13]

It is striking that religious gifts, sometimes seen as extensions of domestic character, were liberally assigned on all sides to the sex which had no professional standing and experienced great difficulty acquiring significant lay power in the national Church. In the Church Congress of 1890, for example, Archdeacon R. F. L. Blunt, after conventional references to woman's physical weakness, her dependent status, and her susceptibility to being 'led astray', after her encounter with the snake in Eden, went on to praise her positive qualities, including greater 'religious instinct' than man. An essentially similar view was expressed by writers in the twentieth century, some of whom were anxious to harness this particular female religious genius for the institutional Church. Thus William Temple, a moderate but definite supporter of the Church women's movement, observed in 1912 that 'women have a greater initial facility for worship than men. It comes to them more easily.' Likewise, Edith Picton-Turbervill, a much more definite feminist than Temple, considered that women possessed a natural mental and spiritual attitude which equipped them 'to hear the voice of God'. A few years later, and from the other side of the ideological divide, the *Church Times* (29 April 1927) simply noted that 'in the sphere of religion woman's greatness is a natural and familiar thing.'[14]

Now and then women expressed themselves in unusual and disturbing ways, and even though their intention was not to challenge but to redefine they expressed woman's conventional role outside the family. Among them Josephine Butler, crusader against the Contagious Diseases Acts, and a committed Anglican, in her introduction to *Woman's Work and Woman's Culture* emphasized a point often made by less assertive personalities: 'A whole family however

---

[13] *Hints to a Clergyman's Wife: or, Female Parochial Duties Practically Illustrated* (London, 1832), 1; Yonge, *Womankind*, p. 188; F. K. Prochaska, *Women and Philanthropy in Nineteenth-century England* (Oxford, 1980), 3.

[14] CCR (1890), 611; William Temple, 'How the Women's Movement May Help the Cause of Religion', in *The Religious Aspect of the Women's Movement* (London, 1912), 58; Edith Picton-Turbervill, *Christ and Woman's Power* (London, 1919), 8.

excellent [does not] do its duty to society by simply
existing. . . . I am sure that the prevailing character of
many homes is only that of a selfishness of five or ten . . .
we are stewards of the manifold gifts of God and stewards
are expected to dispense those gifts to others.'[15]

One vital function within the domestic vocation was
motherhood; it was one much stressed by Victorian church
writers, and given a meaning far beyond natural motherhood. Thus F. E. Paget, author of the *Owlet of Owlstone
Edge*, wrote of the parson's wife 'as adviser, parent,
friend, of young and old; of being . . . "the universal
mother" '. For the Anglo-Catholic Canon Liddon, a major
pastoral problem was how to 'extend, for the benefit of
mankind at large, the active motherly instincts of woman
. . . how to enlarge the bounds of the household assigned
to her by nature'. This theme, the appropriateness of a
maternal character for ladies of community and church
work, was stressed in a contribution by Hesba Stretton to
Baroness Burdett-Coutts's volume on *Woman's Mission* in
1893: 'In all religions which have achieved any wide
sphere of influence, the idea of the mother and child has
been presented as a divine one. The idea almost dominates
the Christian religion . . . therefore, that women should
work for children is as natural as that the sun should shine
on the evil and the good.'[16] Thus did the tradition of
female subordination and the limitations of domesticity
prove flexible; within these very traditional limitations
some women, especially (but not exclusively) well-to-do
ladies, developed spheres of labour in which they were in
fact neither very submissive nor wholly domestic.

The age of subordination did not end with Victoria's
death. Indeed the doctrine remained dominant for many
years and is far from dead yet. But from the last years of

[15] Josephine E. Butler (ed.), *Woman's Work and Woman's Culture: A Series of
Essays* (London, 1869), p. xxxix.
[16] [Francis Edward Paget], *The Owlet of Owlstone Edge: His Travels, His
Experience, and His Lucubrations* (London, 1856), 30; H. P. Liddon, *Phoebe in
London: A Sermon* (London, 1877), 16; Hesba Stretton, 'Women's Work for
Children', in A. Burdett-Coutts (ed.), *Woman's Mission: A Series of Congress Papers
on the Philanthropic Work of Women by Eminent Writers* (London, 1893), 415 (a
report on women's philanthropic work in Britain made for the 1893 Chicago
Exhibition by the Ladies' Committee of the 1851 Royal Commission).

the nineteenth century, indeed, earlier in isolated cases, the orthodoxy of virtually restricting women to the domestic life and of insisting on universal male control was challenged within the Church and among church people. In response to that challenge (which will be considered in Chapter 5) came firmer and shriller affirmations of the traditions of subordination and of domesticity expressed in public church groups, in sermons, and in the Press. On 31 October 1913, for example, the *Church Times* feared that the feminist movement had put such pressure on church forces that 'they may seem to be surrendering to new doctrines striking at the subordination of the sexes [*sic*] and subversive of the reticent delicacy and dignity of womanhood'. It went on to affirm that 'the majority of churchmen refuse to keep an open mind as to the truth of the New Testament about the sexes which has also been the teaching of the Church of all the ages'. In the 1921 Church Congress the redoubtable Canon Sparrow Simpson led off the session on 'Women's Position in the Ministry of the Church' with an address on the principle of subordination. He pronounced that 'the principle of subordination exists in the Church as well as in the home, and there also the man is the head of the woman'.[17] Not content to refer only to the model of Mary, the *Church Times* on 29 April 1927 took up the example of St Monica. 'St. Monica . . . reminds us that much of the most solid work that women do for God comes to them in the course of a normal and purely natural vocation. . . . Monica found her life's work in her motherhood.'

An important variant of the belief in woman's secondary status was the understanding that, although she might be spiritually equal to man in the abstract, in fact she was different in kind, not just different in degree or power. 'It is profoundly true', said Canon J. H. B. Masterman, following Aristotle as well as St Paul, 'that there is a difference between the mind of a man and the mind of a woman, which is quite as pronounced as the physical difference.' Such a view professed to allow 'separate but equal' treatment of men and women, and (its proponents

[17] CCR (1921), 225.

undoubtedly hoped) encouraged the diversion of women's ambitions from contentious areas of contemporary male monopoly in the Church, and also from the dangers of domestic self-assertion. In 1913, the bishop of Southampton addressed a gathering at the time of the Church Congress: 'in certain respects . . . women can never be equal to men, and in other respects it is just as true that men can never be equal to women'. He went on to hope that opportunities would be provided 'for the education of women separately from men to qualify for their own special work'. It transpired, of course, that in the Church, the woman's sphere turned out to exclude vocations of power or direction or, indeed, major ministerial responsibility. In this connection Bishop Charles Gore, generally a supporter of the women's movement, gave cautious but direct support to the doctrine of female subordination. He was convinced of 'fundamental psychological and moral and intellectual differences between men and women' which he believed to be parallel to the evident physical difference between the sexes. When the lives of the two sexes necessarily combined, as in marriage, there must be a superior as well as an inferior partner. Gore thought that 'in an indissoluble partnership I conceive there must always be ultimate headship'. Yet he argued with a wonderful lack of logic that woman's secondary place must involve a 'subordination which . . . involves no inferiority whatever in nature or essence, but only difference of function'.[18] Of course it proved difficult for women who felt called to positions of lay or ministerial church responsibility, but who were rejected for such by the Church on the ground of their distinct sexual character, not to feel inferior. At bottom, church feminism during the first days of the women's movement to about 1930 involved a rejection of the doctrine of subordination, a doctrine which was often jointly expressed in marital and ecclesiastical frameworks.

As the age of subordination extended well into the twentieth century, so the glorification of domesticity and the primacy of home and family in the world of women

---

[18] *Guardian*, 31 Jan. 1913; *Southampton Daily Echo*, 29 Sept. 1913; Charles Gore, in *The Religious Aspect of the Women's Movement*, pp. 34–5.

continued, and was emphasized within the Church by the rapid growth of the Mothers' Union, as well as by a continuing series of statements by clergy and others. In 1908, at the women's meetings of the Pan-Anglican Congress, Louise Creighton, widow of Bishop Mandell Creighton, was in the chair. Although she herself had marked reservations about the traditional view she faithfully noted that 'again and again the *primary* importance of women's work in the home was emphasised', and the summaries of subsequent speeches bear her out. Lady Acland, for example, observed that 'some of us need in these days of great philanthropic activity, to be reminded that our duty to our husband and our children—to our home—does come first, and that no amount of attendance at committees, or organising of bazaar openings, even of such work as district visiting or teaching can make up for a neglected home'. Similar views were expressed in subsequent years in Church congresses and elsewhere.[19] In 1914 Hensley Henson went so far as to assert that 'unmarried women can never be accepted as the true or best representatives of womanhood, however brilliant their intellectual powers, or astonishing their actual achievements'. On the other hand there was a good deal of fear lest the war, by radically expanding women's non-domestic horizons, should have discouraged marriage and motherhood. 'Public opinion must be aroused', wrote a clergyman in 1918, and 'it must go forth as a national cry that "the greatest wish in the world" for a woman married should be to be called "mother".' Such a view was undoubtedly buttressed by a new emphasis on the centrality and skills of motherhood which derived from the child and maternal welfare movement after the beginning of the twentieth century.[20]

One other aspect of the opposition to the women's movement deserves treatment at this stage. Church feminists, like their sisters in politics and elsewhere, wanted power. Whenever it was refused in terms of voice, vote, office, or

[19] *Pan-Anglican Congress of 1908: Report of the Women's Meetings* (London, 1908), vi, 27. See also CCR (1909), 477; *Christian Commonwealth*, 26 June 1912.

[20] *Church Times*, 3 July 1914; *Guardian*, 28 Feb. 1918; Jane Lewis, *The Politics of Motherhood, Child and Maternal Welfare in England, 1900–1939* (London and Montreal, 1980), *passim*.

function, the same sort of justification was put forward. To men alone belonged power; instead women were gifted by God with 'influence'. Influence was really the quality of manipulation. Thus mothers had an enormous influence over their offspring, greatest, of course, when the quality of mothering was at its best. Consequently, when the domestic ideal was most fully realized a woman's influence was greatest over her family.[21] On menfolk the indirect power of a woman's influence could be great indeed: 'they should try to influence their brothers, husbands . . . or friends, to vote for what is right'. Addressing a women's overflow meeting' at the 1902 Church Congress, the Revd R. W. Harris had no trouble agreeing that members of his audience should be 'on Boards of all sorts'. Yet he insisted that 'your real influence does not lie in public life and never will. It lies in the power you exert over men, individually and personally.'[22] Influence was conceived as the real power of fundamentally subordinate and domestic woman.

Despite the radical limitation imposed by the doctrine of female subordination and the sharp restrictions inherent in the domestic ideology, it is remarkable how very much extra-familial work was done by very many churchwomen in late Victorian England, indeed how much of it was achieved under female direction and control (whatever the nominal situation). Most of this activity was voluntary and hugely various in character. It will be considered in the next chapter. There were, however, certain means by which Victorian women could serve the Church on a full-time basis, either as paid workers or as members of a religious order; the significance of these is the subject of Chapter 3. The second part of this book contains four chapters dealing with the rise of the women's movement, a movement determined to change the context of subordination into one of equality.

[21] Burgon, *Woman's Place*, pp. 6–7; CCR (1885), 160; (1886), 472.
[22] CCR (1891), 389; (1902), 449.

2

The Volunteers

IN the last quarter of the nineteenth century the sheer extent of women's participation as volunteer workers was immense, whether in formal societies (auxiliary to male-dominated or immediately directed by women's committees) or as adjuncts to parish or other local organizations. Although it is impossible to place an exact number on this throng, Louisa Hubbard in a chapter in Baroness Burdett-Coutts's *Woman's Mission* (1893) believed 'about half a million are occupied more or less continuously or semi-professionally' in such a fashion.[1] Not only were these unpaid women but they did not include professed sisters or other members of religious orders. Obviously they included many who were not directly connected to religious bodies, much less tied to the national Church in some fashion; yet the religious motive for female phil-anthropy was unquestionably pervasive in late Victorian England. In the words of the Anglo-Catholic bishop of Ohio visiting England in 1878, 'the ruling motive shall always be a True Christian Charity inspired by a devoted love to our Lord'.[2]

No doubt religion was the main moral engine for the great philanthropic surge. But associated with it were others as well. None was more widely held or frequently pressed than the need to use the energies of middle- and upper-class women in appropriate and useful ways. The feeling that such women frittered away their lives was common, especially among leaders of the mid-Victorian pastoral revival. Thus Edward Monro wrote of female 'persons who want a work to employ wasted energies, to give them a recognised place in social and active life, and to find objects on which to bestow strong sympathies and

---

[1] Burdett-Coutts (ed.), *Woman's Mission*, p. 364.
[2] CCR (1878), 342.

yearnings, which otherwise would have no special channel for exhaustion'. Parochial philanthropic work would not only greatly benefit the poor and the pastor but by 'giving them a work and a position' would greatly enhance the lives of lady volunteers. Such enhancement might be valued as providing a serious purpose for life, an answer to those who 'long for something real', aware that 'they are responsible beings approaching an eternity in which they will have to render an account of hours given for higher uses, but spent perhaps on vain trifles'.[3]

On the other hand, volunteer work was sometimes recommended simply as a diversion, 'a welcome relaxation to some women, freed for a time from the cares and little worries of daily duties'. The distinguished pastoral theologian, J. H. Blunt, thought that there were far more ladies of the 'higher and middle class . . . who are at leisure to devote themselves to good works of this kind than there are men of any class and that many of them would gladly fly to them as a relief from compulsory idleness or from occupations of a trivial character'. At least one woman, Mrs Herbert, speaking to a Church congress audience in 1891, adduced patriotic motives for ladies' work with children. 'God [has] . . . given into our hands the training of the race, and if this be so the moral standard will be what we make it . . . remember that every man that goes out from among us helps or hinders God's great purposes of England's rule . . . [Women are] trainers of the race and moral training must have its basis in principle.'[4]

Motives for ladies' involvement in philanthropic work were numerous and overlapping, and they certainly included a desire to protect social stability and enhance the status quo. Certainly many ladies were available. 'Never', said Miss Whately to the Church Congress in 1878, 'in the world's history has there been a time when so many women could be found possessed of leisure and in a position to devote the whole or the chief part of their time to work in the Lord's vineyard.'[5]

[3] E. Monro, *Parochial Work* (London, 1850), 168.
[4] CCR (1895), Mrs Chute; Blunt, *Directorium Pastorale*, p. 325. CCR (1891), 387.
[5] See Prochaska, *Women and Philanthropy*, pp. 102–3; CCR (1878), Miss Whately.

Frances Cobbe elaborated somewhat on the 'natural-ness' of these keenly-pursued appointments.

Whatever else may be doubtful . . . it is pretty well conceded that she [woman] is in her right place teaching the young, reclaiming the sinful, relieving the poor, and nursing the sick . . . also, on the part of women themselves, there is a tendency, in nine out of ten, to choose one or other line of benevolent action rather than any path of science, art, or learning.[6]

Frank Prochaska's *Women and Philanthropy in Nineteenth-century England* demonstrates much of the width, variety, and volume of women's philanthropic activity; their money-raising activities, their domestic, institutional, and occupational visitations, and their special concern with 'rescue' work and the purity movement. What he describes as the 'inescapable importance of religion' in all this is far from confined to the importance of the Church of England. Nevertheless, the Established Church was a major focus of female volunteer activity. Thousands upon thousands of ladies attached themselves, in duly subordinate capacities, to thousands of parish priests, as district visitors, Sunday School teachers, and patrons and organizers of local charities. Thousands more became involved in the world of missionary and other societies. A huge number joined societies, founded and organized by churchwomen themselves, to elevate the lives and ideal of women and children. In her preface to *Woman's Mission* (1893) Baroness Burdett-Coutts listed the 'Churches of England, Ireland and Scotland; the Moravian Church; the Presbyterian Church of Scotland; the Roman Catholic Church; Congregational organisations; the Jewish communion, [and] the Society of Friends' as 'the largest philanthropic organizations whose branches are scattered throughout the world'. Writing in the same work, Mrs Boyd Carpenter pointed to the advantage of the parochial system in organizing philanthropy; if adhered to, it prevented the same charity duplicating its role in the same territory, while direction from the local parish priest prevented local

6 F. P. Cobbe, *Essay on the Pursuits of the Churches* (London, 1863), 105.

rivalries from developing. Furthermore, multi-parish units (such as rural deaneries) meant that parochial cures too small to have their own branches of a charity would have an administrative unit from which to function.[7]

Of the estimated half-million philanthropic volunteer women workers in the latter decades of the century, several hundred thousand certainly worked directly under Church of England auspices. Of these, several thousand were members of the clergy families, wives, daughters, or sisters. James Obelkevich pointed out that in Lincolnshire in the 1870s 'in many parishes the only lay assistants were the wife and daughters of the parson who complacently described them as doing all that was necessary'. Certainly a review of the literature earlier in the century demonstrates the extent of the demand upon clergy women, especially clergy wives. The anonymous *Hints to a Clergyman's Wife* (1832) was particularly insistent. The author evidently thought of marriage to a clergyman as simultaneous commitment to his vocation; 'nothing connected with her can be neutral'. In particular she would be expected to visit the poor assiduously, first to assess the state of the parish, later, through 'more systematic visits, to learn of each family intimately, to encourage their day and Sunday Schools, to point out to them . . . their relative duties and give available advice as to domestic economy, diligence, frugality, and order', as well as to inculcate 'habits of self-denial, industry and cleanliness'. The object was to 'promote a cheerful, contented disposition and lead them to look at the bright side even of those little adverse circumstances which are perpetually occuring in this changing and uncertain world'. The poor 'often need to be reminded that happiness belongs to a cottage no less than to a palace; that it depends upon character rather than upon circumstances'.[8]

As if this vast and continuing project were not enough, the clergyman's wife should also take fundamental responsi-

[7] Prochaska, *Women and Philanthropy, passim*; Mrs Boyd Carpenter, 'Women's Work in Connection with the Church of England', in Burdett-Coutts (ed.), *Woman's Mission*, p. 114.

[8] James Obelkevich, *Religion and Rural Society: South Lindsey, 1825–1875* (Oxford, 1976), 178–9; *Hints to a Clergyman's Wife*, pp. 50, 56, 58, 59.

bility for female schools as 'superintendent' and indeed substitute for her allegedly overworked husband in the 'direction and occasional inspection' of the entire parochial education system. The same author also encouraged her to provide 'cottage readings' for poor women, to organize a 'sewing school' for one or two evenings a week, and even to attempt a sort of employment agency for humble wives who could spin or knit to supplement the family income.[9]

All this raised a problem which could well become painful and pointed. To what extent must wives (and, when appropriate, daughters and sisters) be partners in their men's ministry? How much was such free public service expected? To what degree could it be sustained by wives who were also mothers of large families? In modern sociological jargon, to what degree should a Victorian clerical wife expect to be 'incorporated' into her husband's profession?

In the early and mid-Victorian literature, clerical wives were usually pictured as having a vocation in common with their husbands' as 'fellow labourers in their Master's vineyard'. The women of the vicarage were said to 'make the clergyman's efficiency double what it would otherwise be and in some instances increase it ten fold'. Nevertheless, it had to be made clear that the ladies of the rectory were not in any way church officials, vying for place with their husbands. Charlotte Yonge put it very simply: the clergyman's wife must remember that she is not the clergyman. In the 1890s others reiterated this point: Mrs Creighton, very active herself as an incumbent's and later a bishop's wife, wrote that 'she [the parson's wife] has a sphere, but it is an entirely subordinate one, more subordinate than that of any other wife'.[10]

Although having no 'official position' it was perfectly clear to end-of-century observers such as Charles Booth that the role of vicarage women was vital in the metropolis; among these women 'there is no figure . . . more beautiful than that of the woman who as wife or

[9] *Hints to a Clergyman's Wife*, pp. 80, 124, 160, 163.
[10] Ibid, p. 187; Louise Creighton, *Life and Letters of Mandell Creighton* (London, 1904), i. 5, 8.

daughter faithfully shares her husband's or father's parish work'. The theme of joint vocation persisted. In the Church Assembly of 1927, a Mrs Moore of Lincoln reminded her audience that 'the wife of no other professional man was expected to take such a part in her husband's job'. Clerical wives were described simply as 'unpaid curates'. In 1932, Dora Freestone wrote un-ashamedly in her *An Ideal Minister's Wife* that 'the wife is just as much a necessity to the Church as the minister himself', and the home must take 'second place' to the parish. Her duties must include attendance at services, mothers' meetings, social work, and Sunday School activity. She must be a 'good organizer', 'a good visitor', and a 'good student' (in order to 'discuss the latest books with her husband'). Such were what one woman speaker at the end of Victoria's reign called 'the duties, the responsibilities and obligations of our vocation as clergy wives of the Church of England'. This was the tradition which provoked Mrs Richardson to refer to clergy wives as 'clergywomen' in her book *Women of the Church of England* published in 1907. One such individual was Mrs Kingsley, Charles Kingsley's mother who in St Luke's, Chelsea, had 'established an ascendancy that she was never to relinquish. With parochial schools and Bible classes and district visitors to manage, she had at last found scope for her organizing abilities and she took over the running of the parish without hesitation.' More attractive is the picture of the Edwardian Mrs Baillie sketched by her daughter in the *Autobiography of a Decade* (1958), an extraordinarily warm-hearted, cultured, and humble woman, who with constant affection and good cheer supported her husband in a slum ministry.[11]

Against this persistent and dominant theme of co-operation—through subordination and parish vocations for wives, daughters, and sisters of the parsonage—a different view gradually emerged. At first it contrasted the domestic role of vicarage ladies and the need to protect

[11] Booth, *Religious Influences*, vii. 25; RP Ch. Assoc. (1927), viii. 249; Dora Freestone, *An Ideal Minister's Wife* (London, 1932), 8–12, 79; Mrs Aubrey Richardson, *Women of the Church of England* (London, 1907), 260 ff.; E. Baillie, *The Shabby Paradise: The Autobiography of a Decade* (London, 1958), 100 ff.

them from undue parochial demands. Later it tentatively gave some importance to their rights as independent human beings separate from their menfolks' professional concerns.

Early in the Victorian period, Elizabeth Pierce, author of *Village Pencillings* (1842), had put much emphasis on the 'aimiable and gentle wife' whose duties were primarily domestically supportive and exemplary, and only indirectly professionally helpful. Others placed weight on the 'clergy woman's' power of example, a model Christian wife and housewife, 'looked upon as adviser, parent, friend, of young and old; of being "the universal mother" '. Rather than actually lead in the parochial work of the parish, 'she best helps her husband by not engaging in all the works of the parish . . . she best helps her husband by looking well to the ways of her own household. The parish priest's family should be a model one. He has no time to make it so himself and therefore he must leave it to his wife.' At the 1896 Church Congress an extended discussion revolved around the duties of a clergyman's wife; and several expressed the opinion that 'the first duty of her life must be the home', although most continued to saddle her with much parochial leadership. It was recognized by one speaker that public work in the parish did not form a part of their pastoral vocation: 'some of us . . . must be content to sit on the back bench'. [12]

The tendency to differentiate between matrimonial and domestic support and parochial partnership grew in the twentieth century as servants disappeared from parsonages, thereby condemning more parsons' wives to more hours of household drudgery. Wives themselves began to sense a greater degree of independence from their spouses. A warm correspondence on this subject developed in the summer of 1917 in the conservative and rather High Church *Guardian*. It was set off by a clergy wife who asked the question point blank. 'Is a parson's wife under any greater obligation to qualify as her husband's assistant than the wife of a doctor or any other professional man? In a word, is she a Rectoress or a Vicaress, or is she merely

[12] Elizabeth Pierce, *Village Pencillings* (London, 1842), 78; Paget, *The Owlet of Owlstone Edge*, p. 30; CCR (1873), Sir James Phipps; CCR (1896), 333 ff.

the wife of a man who happens to be a Rector or a Vicar?' The ensuing correspondence represented a wide spectrum of opinion on the matter of 'incorporation', with most admitting (but not necessarily approving) the fact that 'she has come to be regarded as a spiritual beast of burden'. The last letter, from the wife of a retired vicar, on 30 September 1917, asserted firmly that 'My absolutely first duty was to my home, my husband, and my children. . . . I am absolutely certain that the reason so many of their [clergymen's] children grow up ungodly is because the mother has put parish first and children second.'[13]

No doubt the clergy wives (and resident daughters and sisters) remained important, probably pivotal factors, in the volunteer battalions of the parochial Church of England structure. There is no question that they played a vital role from mid-Victorian times well into the 1930s, as they still do. However, it is equally clear that the onset of the twentieth century brought with it an occasion of doubt about combining domestic and parochial female leadership in the first lady of the vicarage. More and more people were seeing the need for a disinterested and trained female parish worker, taking Mrs Creighton's view (expressed in 1901) that 'the clergyman's wife has no offical position. Her first duty must always be to her husband and children and she will help her husband in his work best by so ordering her home that he may always find it a place of rest and refreshment, and by so bringing up her children and managing her household that his home may be an example of what a Christian home should be.' Clergy wives remained, for the most part, subordinate servants of the Church, 'unpaid curates', a peculiar species of constrained volunteers. Yet by 1930, it was hardly an unquestioned assumption that a woman who married a parson became his parochial assistant, nor that a female born into a clergyman's family, if she remained unmarried, might well expect to spend her life doing the parochial work of her father or her brother.[14]

13 RP Ch. Assoc. (1927), viii, no. 2, p. 249; *Guardian*, 2 Aug. 1917; *National News*, 30 Sept. 1917.
14 Louise Creighton, 'The Work of Women in the Parish', in *Laity in Council. Essays in Ecclesiastical and Social Problems. By Lay Members of the Anglican*

'Clergywomen' certainly provided the focus for much female volunteer work at the parochial level towards the end of the nineteenth century, and indeed well into the twentieth century. But around that focus, certainly around the parochial parish centre, clustered very large groups of volunteer ladies of which numerically the most important were parochial district visitors. Numbers are hard to come by before 1889, and even then no distinctions were made in the *Official Year-book of the Church of England* between male and female district visitors. In that year, a table which 'represents the work of 80% of the parishes in England and Wales' reveals 47,112 district visitors, undoubtedly mostly female. In 1909–10, the number listed for the Church as a whole was 74,009, a figure which increased to 76,249 in 1916–17 but declined to 74,647 in 1918. By 1928 despite a steady decline in numbers district visitors were still listed at 64,173, more than during the late 1860s. However suspect or accurate these figures may turn out to be, other evidence seems to demonstrate the large extent of participation, particularly female participation, in widespread philanthropy. In Baroness Burdett-Coutts's book, Mrs Boyd Carpenter wrote in 1893 of at least two or three women in each English or Welsh parish who were involved in this work. A few years later Charles Booth wrote of a parish in London with thirty-five district visitors 'all living within parishes, being the wives and sisters of our working people'. In February 1917, Emily Wilding Davison mentioned the figure of 85,000 district visitors of whom 75,000 she said, were women. Whatever the exact numbers, observers were aware of a vast volunteer enterprise, predominantly female in composition, clearly forming a major part of late Victorian women's 'church work' and persisting well into the twentieth century.[15]

One familiar principle which informed all Anglican district visiting within the Victorian and Edwardian period was

Communion. Edited by J. H. Burn (London, 1901), 187; See also CCR (1899), Mrs Lyttelton, and L. S. Hunter, *A Parson's Job* (London, 1931), p. 210.

[15] *The Official Year-book of the Church of England* (hereafter cited as *Church of England Year-book*) (1889), *passim*; (1917), 404; (1918), 408; Boyd Carpenter in Burdett-Coutts (ed.), *Woman's Mission*, p. 113.

that of subordination to the parish priest. This is very clear from the handbooks of pastoral theology written expressly for the new-style incumbents, more 'professional' and perhaps less diffuse in their vocations than their eighteenth-century predecessors. In a pre-Victorian work, *The District Visitors' Handbook* (1820), there is evidence of a clergyman named Israel Saunders who 'divided his parish into districts chiefly to allow teachers to visit Sunday School parents'. He evidently started a District Visitors' Society in his parish in 1829. Other clerical advisers took the view that efficiently organized and duly subordinate district visitors in every parish would reach the poor and allow the incumbent to 'concentrate his energies on that part of his work which cannot be delegated to another—the administration of the sacraments, the preaching of the word, and the pastoral visitation of the sick and dying'. Over and over again throughout the Victorian period the district visitors—usually thought of as ladies with leisure time to give to the Church—and the parish priest, were considered co-operators.[16] The women's function, as seen by all, was nicely summarized by the Revd Harry Jones of London as sweeping 'the work up towards the chief'. No opportunity was neglected to point out their position with respect to the clerical professional man in the parish. Thus, although the form of local organization seemed to have become that of a parochial Visiting Society, the work and organization, in Anglican circles, was always subordinate and obedient to clergymen of the parish. Unless this were the case, 'there would be confusion and evil'. As Charles Bridges put it in *The Christian Ministry* (1834), 'it was never intended that the minister should sustain the whole weight of the service of God'. Even so, 'a spirit of independency . . . [with] the consequent diminution of the just influence of the Parochial Head' must be avoided.

Why did such a large number of women function as pastoral auxiliaries in this way? What moved the parochial lady to volunteer as a district visitor under conditions of such complete subordination? It would surely be an error to discount the frequently alleged and straightforward

16 *The District Visitors' Handbook* (London, 1820), 40.

religious motives for women taking up this service. 'Let your highest motive be the constraining love of Christ . . . and the reward you look forward to . . . his approbation', wrote the author of *Hints to District Visitors* in 1858, and there is no reason to think that such was not the case. At the end of the century, the highest motive was 'to help others to know the love of our Lord Jesus Christ'; this was held up as the proper spur to the task, the supreme necessity of the spiritual life, and the true spiritual aim in the visitor herself. Well into the Edwardian period Arthur Jephson wrote that 'to turn people from darkness to light . . . from the power of Satan unto God' was a visitor's chief motive. But this sacred/secular line was becoming somewhat blurred, and Jephson was fulsome in advising and demonstrating to those who were visited how they 'may become better and more useful Church-people and citizens'. Clearly, between the purely religious motives and the variety of secular reasons for visiting lay the pastoral imperative which has already been discussed: the need to evangelize and care for the poor. Not only was this seen by the parish priest as a motive for adopting a visiting system, but also by the visitor as a reason for taking up the task. Thus an anonymous writer asserted that it 'represents a desire on the part of those who have . . . spare time to help their clergy to bear the great burden of responsibility which is laid on the care of the parish'. The more precisely secular motivations became clearer towards the end of the nineteenth century, although, as Frank Prochaska has shown, they certainly existed from the time of the French Revolution. Even William Cadman, the great London Evangelical pastor, wrote in 1873 of the 'help of the Christian females' as district visitors exerting 'an influence untold upon cleanliness and sobriety, and industrious habits, upon parochial authority and filial obedience and social kindness', and the historian Roger Lloyd has described early twentieth-century district visitors as generally 'more amateur welfare workers than laywomen consciously exercising the priesthood of the laity'.

Of course, the instruction a visitor might probably dispense should be in line with the appropriate feminine

ideals, conformity to 'the model of all purity, the Blessed Virgin Mary [who] dwelt in a cottage home' so that 'any sort of feminine employment that tends to interest girls and to make them "keepers at home" would be taught . . . all ideas of money-making and prize winning should be carefully excluded'. Thus the sense of self-fulfilment on the part of the agent was to be united in the spread of the Victorian Christian female ideal among the underprivileged.

Usually, district visiting was an activity of the leisured classes and was directed towards the poor. It was also an activity which required definite personal qualities. One was the capacity to make friends in the homes of the poor. In *Visiting* (1906), Ada Vachell wrote, 'The great secret of visiting . . . is making friends.' She went on, 'only when you are a "friend" can you give without hurting, can you proffer advice which there is a chance of being accepted . . . have you the authority or right to reprove'. Friendship is seen by Vachell as a 'lever'. A similar quality was emphasized many years before by the author of *Hints on District Visiting* (1877): only women without children and families of their own could concentrate adequately on other families and the poor in the neighbourhood. In his pastoral counsel, the author of *Hints* recommended that the age of a visitor be twenty-five or over, that she have a good domestic record of her own, and that she have a deep personal 'knowledge of the Faith'. The importance of personal qualities is emphasized in virtually every handbook of district visiting. Not uncommon is the sense of service felt by superiors towards inferiors, stressed by the Master of the Temple in 1840, who drew the parallel of Christ washing the feet of His disciples.[17] Late-Victorian,

[17] Harry Jones, *Priest and Parish* (London, 1866), 67; Charles Bridges, *The Christian Ministry; With an Inquiry into the Causes of its Inefficiency, and with an Especial Reference to the Ministry of the Establishment*,6th edn. (London, 1864), 473; *Hints to District Visitors* (London, 1858), 17; Arthur Jephson, *Some Hints for Parish Workers in London* (London, 1904), 4–5; Prochaska, *Women and Philanthropy*, p. 102; 'F. C.', *A Talk About District Visiting* (London, 1895), 3; William Cadman, *Lay Helpers* (London, 1873), 46; Roger Lloyd, *The Church of England 1900–1965* (London, 1966), 162; Clement Rogers, *Principles of Parish Work* (London, 1905); Booth, *Religious Influences*, p. 33; Ada Vachell, *Visiting* (London, 1906), 5; *Hints on District Visiting* (London, 1877), 7–9; C. Benson, in *District Visitors Manual* (London, 1840), 19.

but common to the entire period, is the advice in *Lay Help in District Visiting* by Elizabeth Harcourt Mitchell, who wrote in 1899 that the need for a spiritual basis for district visiting, as well as the careful adjustment of the spiritual/ secular mix and the extreme importance of courtesy, was 'the very first thing required' when dealing with the poor. She insisted that there should be two important elements in visiting. First of all, she recommended that the visitor should be actively 'loyal to the priest', a very important aspect; while on the other hand she should consult the feelings of the poor and demonstrate a real 'sympathy' for them. Mitchell also gave practical advice, such as how many families (twenty to thirty) should be assigned to each visitor and how many visits should be made in one session (seven). Along with the qualities required for the district visitor the dangers to which district visiting might lead were always listed. Very often these were simply the antitheses of the qualities desired in district visitors. For example, J. Llewelyn Davies wrote in 1855 that one should always avoid being 'intrusive' in the homes of the poor, that one should avoid 'becoming a mere dispenser of relief . . . we must not turn any poor persons into hungry animals'. The warnings were taken up later in the century, for example by the Oxford Clerical Association in 1862 and by the *Guardian* on 17 November 1858, which warned that 'it is common to begin by putting a whole string of queries, suggested in some manual, in a dry abrupt manner, accompanied perhaps by the strictures on the cleanliness of the cottage, inquisitorial prying into the dinner being provided for the family, lectures on the duty of going to Church, hints on the propriety of immigration' and con- cluding with a distribution of tracts. The effect, warns the *Guardian* is 'immense . . . alienation between the classes . . . increased, and the deplorable impression that the gentry do not consider them as of the same flesh and blood with themselves'. There is a very real need to be seen as 'equals',

to show an acquaintance with sympathy for their peculiar trials, and personal attention to their wants; to let them see that we do regard them as fellow-beings, as having the same feelings, the same sources of joy and sorrow, as ourselves, and the same right to share of the enjoyments as well as the necessaries of life.

Thus the dangers and problems of district visiting were recognized as fully as were the advantages and possibilities. If some of the skills of the successful district visitor were innate, a matter of individual personality, some were to be learned, and, particularly towards the end of the century, the learned skills were emphasized in books of pastoral theology. Thus 'F. C.' in *A Talk About District Visiting* (1895) described a proper visit as one with a purpose, one accompanied by a 'bright manner,' one in which the visitor dressed well and in which he or she displayed 'courtesy at all times'. He noted in this book that 'a woman's heart is alike in all ranks'. He warned against visiting at inconvenient times and he insisted that the visitor listen 'patiently and tenderly' to the person visited. He insisted that the visitor know how to 'pray aloud' and do so in an extemporaneous manner when this was called for.[18]

Contemporaries had no doubt of the need for trained parish visitors, but they must be very carefully prepared if they were to be of real use to the parish priest. The volume published in 1893 by Lady Jeune included an article by Sophia Lonsdale entitled 'Women's Work Amongst the Poor', which warned about the inadequacies of the younger clergy and also of many ladies.

What is true of the young clergy is equally true of other workers. A girl has time on her hands, she hears that District Visitors are wanted in her parish, she wishes to do something for Christ's poor and His Church, her offer of help is accepted . . . most of her ideas about the poor are taken from descriptions in magazines, where speaker and misery are pictured in the 'darkest colours', their ignorance as to trades, rates and wages, the Poor Law, and the agencies available for relief is complete. To put it shortly, she has no true idea of the real position of the people among whom she is to work.

The only cure for this, wrote Miss Lonsdale, was previous instruction from other experienced visitors, and clergy also

[18] Elizabeth Harcourt Mitchell, *Lay Help in District Visiting* (London, 1899), 7–13; J. Llewelyn Davies, *District Visiting* (London, 1855), 124–9; Bodl. MSS Oxford Clerical Assoc., xi. 44; 'F. C.', *A Talk About District Visiting*, pp. 10–12.

perhaps, acquired at Charity Organization Society meetings at which she should be a regular attender.[19] Similarly, Louise Creighton, wife of Bishop Mandell Creighton, in her article 'The Work of Women in the Parish' in *Laity in Council*, wrote of the need for trained parish workers, and at a Church Conference in 1899 she remarked, 'it is curious to compare an article which appeared some thirty years ago in the *Saturday Review*, on the District Visitor, with the ideal sketched by Miss Sewell in her paper on the subject, which every District Visitor should study. But the District Visitor of the past is very far from extinct, and it is hard to see how we are to find those who will realise the ideal of the present.'[20]

Beyond a doubt, Sunday School teaching in the nineteenth century was a widespread form of female volunteer activity within the Church of England and beyond it. In his *Ordination Lectures* of 1862 Bishop Henry MacKenzie believed there were 300,000 such teachers in England and Wales 'far exceeding the army, navy and police of the whole kingdom'. Presumably this estimate is for the Church alone, in which case it seems somewhat high when compared with later estimates. Some twenty years later the total number of Protestant Sunday School teachers in England and Wales was placed at over half a million teaching five million Sunday School scholars. In the first Church statistics with recognized reliability, which appeared in the *Official Year-book of the Church of England* for 1883, 113,412 teachers are listed for 58 per cent of all Church of England parishes (8,405 in England and Wales). Some 42 per cent had not sent in returns. Presumably this would mean that there were over 100,000 women teachers in all parishes together. The 1889 *Year-book* listed 91,642 female teachers in English and Welsh parishes. In 1910 the *total* number of teachers, both male and female (49 per cent of the parishes) is listed as 215,354. Sketchy and

---

[19] Lady Jeune, Introduction in *Ladies at Work* (London, 1893); Harcourt Mitchell, *Lay Help in District Visiting*, 3 ff.; Sophia Lonsdale, 'Women's Work Amongst the Poor' in Lady Jeune, *Ladies at Work* (London, 1893), 129–30.

[20] Louise Creighton, in *Laity in Council*, 119 ff. and 'The Training of Women Church Workers', CCR (1899), 130.

dubious as such figures are, they do show that this form of volunteer church work was popular among the Church of England lay women in the nineteenth century and beyond.[21]

It was widely accepted in Victorian England that religious training was an extension of domesticity, an essential part of the process of child-rearing for which women were created. This was clearly expressed in the paper presented at the Pan-Anglican Congress held in 1908; mothers were seen as 'the earliest teachers of religion for almost the whole of early childhood'. It was through them that children grasped the idea of God, their sense of religious duty, their basic knowledge of Holy Scripture.[22] The domestic woman, the ideal woman, could extend her religious nurturing power beyond school through to the Sunday School. In an article entitled 'The Sunday School as a Sphere of Influence', a writer in the *Guardian* (12 September 1918) pointed out that

the woman or girl who is obliged to remain at home . . . is apt to feel that she is in a blind alley . . . and she becomes restless and dissatisfied . . . who can blame a woman who wishes to make for herself a bigger world, even if not far from home, a field of greater usefulness? To the woman living at home, with a couple of spare hours a day and an absolutely free Sunday comes . . . the call of taking up Sunday School teaching.

Willingness was not enough and over the years there was a good deal of adverse criticism of the amateur help which staffed the Sunday Schools of the national Church. In 1855 the author of *Women and Their Work* quoted Florence Nightingale: 'how usual it is to see families, with five or six daughters at home, with no other occupation in life than a class in Sunday School: and that is that—a Chapter of the Bible is opened at random and the spiritual doctor, with no more idea of her patient's malady than she has plans for improving it, explains at random'. In 1871, the author of *Sunday Schools: Their Use and Abuse*, a reforming work, gave a dark picture of the contemporary

[21] Henry MacKenzie, *Ordination Lectures* (London, 1862), 89; Chadwick, *The Victorian Church*, ii. 257; *Church of England Year-book* (1883), 210–11.

[22] Helena L. Powell, *Women as Teachers of Religion* in *Pan-Anglican Papers* (London, 1908), 35.

scene in which, 'children . . . are collected an hour or an hour and a half before Church time, kept in stiff order, often in a close room, crammed by incompetent teachers with information most liberal in quantity, most deficient in quality; afterwards they are taken to Church. In the afternoon more school.' No wonder, he went on, that 'too often our scholars, as soon as they arrive at the years of discretion, throw off school and Church-going together'. The low opinion of Sunday School persisted, despite vigorous efforts to upgrade both the agents and materials of instruction, so that by 1905 Clement Rogers in his *Principles of Parish Work* discerned what he frankly called 'the complete failure of our Sunday Schools' and wrote of them as the childhood substitutes for unselfconscious church-going which might otherwise have marked the lives of the working class. Certainly twentieth-century statistics of Sunday School attendance seem to bear out the pessimistic view of the Schools. Despite the substantial and continuous rise in population, the Church of England's Sunday School teachers declined from about 215,351 in the period 1907–14 to about 169,304 in the early 1920s and roughly 165,167 in the period 1929–35. It is claimed that educational growth in the nineteenth century was followed by a decline during and after World War I, both in numbers attending Church of England Sunday Schools and in the numbers who taught them.[23]

The late-Victorian growth in Church Sunday Schools and consequently in women's volunteer work in them was much stimulated by the perceived decline in church attendance which had such an influence over working-class elementary education after 1870. Not only the loss of Church control but the general decline of Christian training and the competition of secular knowledge spurred on advocates of Sunday Schools in the later nineteenth century.[24] Over this increasingly popular development the parish priest was himself to preside, both controlling

[23] *Women and Their Work* (London, 1855), 8, quoting a pamphlet by Florence Nightingale; *Sunday Schools: Their Use and Abuse* (London, 1871), 4; Clement Rogers, *Principles of Parish Work* (London, 1905), 224; *Church of England Year-book* (1911), (1923), (1930).

[24] See James Kay-Shuttleworth, Introduction in Louise M. Hubbard, *Work for Ladies in Elementary Schools* (London, 1872).

teachers and sometimes meeting directly with the
scholars. Ashton Oxendon wrote, 'to keep the Sunday
School teachers together and to sustain their interest in
their work a Clergyman should meet with them monthly
to discuss the forthcoming lessons'. The controlling role of
the parish priest was frequently emphasized at the end
of the century. In May 1882 the Bishop of Ely spoke for
'the staff of male and female catechists [assisting the
clergymen], acting in subordination to himself, and under
his supervision' or, as he also remarked, the first principle
of Sunday School organization must be that 'the parish
priest must regard it as *his* Sunday School by virtue of his
office as the appointed catechist of the children within his
bounds. He should not only teach in it himself, but cause
the Sunday School teachers to regard themselves as his
deputies.'[25]

Women volunteer teachers were thus to work under the
parish priest. Despite the moans of critics, real efforts were
made to assist him and to train his teachers. The chief agency
through which the priest got help in training his teachers was
the Church of England Sunday School Institute, founded in
1843, with over 8,000 clergy affiliated twenty years later
and some 300 local associations. This organization gave
assistance through developing and managing its 'visitors',
provided quantities of literature and teaching material,
and, probably more important, established teacher-training
classes and teachers' examinations. In 1881, 994 candidates
for the latter were examined of whom only about 13 per
cent failed.[26] It is evident that the problem of preparation
in developing standards in Sunday School education was
in the minds of some churchmen long before 1900. With
the surge of concern for training at the turn of the century,
this was even more apparent. The Revd W. Hugh Campbell
in the *Guardian* of 25 April 1918 expressed his belief that
full-time lay women workers were required to increase the
knowledge of volunteer Sunday School teachers and to
make them aware of appropriate teaching methods. About

[25] Ashton Oxendon, *The Pastoral Office* (London, 1857), 197; *Church of England Year-book* (1883), 199, 202.
[26] *Church of England Year-book* (1883), 207–9.

ten years before the Sunday School Institute was established, a training-college at Blackheath was founded for
this purpose, initially providing a one-year course in theological education, with supervised training and discussion.
By 1918 'nearly 200 women' had taken the course; of these
sixteen held appointments over the area of a Diocese, one
worked through two archdeaconries, two through rural
deaneries, and the others organized schools in individual
parishes. Earning about £100 each a year their purpose
was to enable 'amateurs' to function effectively in a
traditionally volunteer role. This sort of support for the
unpaid volunteer took other forms in the 1920s, even as
the extent of Sunday Schools themselves diminished. One
such was the week-long summer school for Sunday School
teachers to 'honour' the teachers, provide family recreation
for them, and 'to provide them all with the chance of
improving their knowledge and methods'. The *Church
Times* reflected that the summer schools were important to
the cause of 'the Proletarian Sunday School' which
'helped to insure the Christian Truth being taught to our
English children in town and country in place of a Red Flag
and Marxism doctrine'.[27] Although vastly reduced in
extent in post-war years, the importance of the Sunday
School volunteer increased as a result of the continuing,
and indeed growing, concern about training amateur staff.
In 1934 the total number of Church of England Sunday
scholars is listed as only 1,697,607 (compared to a high
point of 2,561,520 in 1911–12), and the staff of teachers
were reduced to 154,120 (from a twentieth-century peak of
over 220,000 just before the war): the numbers of women
emphasized the fact that the recognition and training of a
good volunteer Sunday School staff was still an essential
part of parochial work.[28]

Mrs Boyd Carpenter in *Woman's Mission* wrote in 1893 of
the advantages of the parish system for philanthropy. She
remarked on three particular advantages: first, the parish
system prevents over-lapping, for the Church covers all

[27] *Church Times*, 31 August 1923.
[28] *Church of England Year-book* (1913), *passim*.

the Christians in the area at once; second, the rural
deanery composed of several parishes makes possible 'a
centre for reaching out to serve parishes which are too
small to have a branch of their own of the philanthropic
cause in question'; third, the parish system prevents
rivalries, for work must have the 'sanction and support
of the local cleric'.[29] Thus, as Frank Prochaska writes,
philanthropy was 'the leisured woman's most obvious
outlet for self-expression'. Philanthropy found expression
both in organizations run by women themselves and in
agencies which were adjuncts to men's organizations.
Many of the original District Visiting Societies were in fact
women's societies and spanned various parishes.[30] In
addition, there were organizations for mothers and girls
which will shortly be considered, as well as societies for
immigration (such as the British Ladies Immigration
Association), for children, and the White Cross Army for
rescue work. Some women's work was of a voluntary kind
and very modest in nature, such as that involving the introduction of needlework to the poor. It is doubtful, however, if the work of any of these organizations approached
the extent of participation in parochial charity.[31] One area
of importance was the co-operation between men and
women in the women's committee of the Church of England
Temperance Society. Dr Scharlieb, one of the early women
physicians, spoke at length in the Church Congress of 1894
about the Society and about the work of temperance
among women. In 1890 there were approximately 4,000
members in this Women's Union and many objectives
were listed. They included that of temperance reading in
Mothers' Meetings and also the establishment of public
houses for the dissemination of coffee rather than liquor.
This was one of the main objects of the remarkable Bee

[29] Boyd Carpenter, 'Women's Work in Connection with the Church of
England' in Burdett-Coutts (ed.), *Woman's Mission*, pp. 114–15.

[30] Frank Prochaska, 'Women in English Philanthopy, 1790–1830' in *International Review of Social History*, 19 (1974), 426–45.

[31] See Mrs Stuart Wortley, 'Emigration', in Burdett-Coutts (ed.), *Woman's
Mission*, p. 87; Burdett-Coutts, p. 11; Prochaska, *Women and Philanthropy*, p. 215;
Mrs J. A. Sala, 'Workers in Guilds and Work Societies', in Burdett-Coutts,
pp. 72 ff.

Hankey's organization patronized by Canon Raven. In 1912 she established an organization known as the 'Catch-My-Pals'. As Charles Raven later wrote, 'drink was the great evil that Help [i.e. Beatrice Hankey] tackled, and not only did she start the Pals, but after many talks and interviews with authorities she did do something towards opening their eyes to the terrible evils of the clubs, where men and women would drink and lie about in sodden heaps, never leaving the place through the holiday week-ends'.[32]

Much has been made of the activity of women and children in raising money for the mission field. Certainly 'in the years following 1866, branches of the Ladies' Association [of the Society for the Propagation of the Gospel] were formed in many home dioceses, the aim being that at least every parish that supported the S.P.G. should also support the Ladies' Association and that subscribers to the Society should understand that if women's work were to be supplied in the Missions, the Association as well as the society must be fed with money'.[33] 'In the year ending March 1897 no less than 400 women's meetings were . . . held in various parts of the country: addresses were also given in 150 schools; and 3,000 copies of a "Terminal Letter" to school-girls had been sent out each term.' The general effectiveness of auxiliaries in the mission field will be discussed in Part II; it is sufficient here to note that G. A. Gollock in 1900 questioned the effectiveness of an existing committee of a monthly character. Even fund-raising became a competitive enterprise. 'The more strange and unnecessary appeared the division of interest between the women's work and the general work of the society [the SPG] the greater the likelihood of an appearance of rivalry between the two organizations for the collection of funds.'[34]

[32] Charles E. Raven and Rachel F. Heath, *One Called Help: The Life and Work of Beatrice Hankey* (London, 1937), 135; Dr Scharlieb, in CCR, (1894), 245; see *Church of England Annual Report* (1890), for the Church of England Temperance Society and the Women's Union.

[33] Ellen F. Humphry, *Ministries of Women During Fifty Years in Connection with the S.P.G.* (London, 1915), 5–10.

[34] Eugene Stock, *The History of the Church Missionary Society*, iii (1899), 695; G. A. Gollock, 'Memorandum on Reconstruction of the Women's Department', 27 Feb. 1900, Church Missionary Society Archives, London: G. AC4/30/5939; Humphry, *Ministries of Women*, p. 19.

If drink and missions were two areas in which women participated with men in the work of the Church, the activities of mothers and girls were areas in which women had a unique part all to themselves. Thus the Mothers' Union and the Girls' Friendly Society were especially important in the life of the Victorian and Edwardian Churches. In 1874 Mrs Townsend, founder of the GFS, outlined three purposes for the Society: 'the preservation of purity,' the distinctive aim of the GFS throughout its life; 'the prevention of moral evil,' that is to say a forward-looking moral aim; and 'the promotion of friendship'. The late Victorian and Edwardian growth of the society was remarkable, but the eve of the First World War proved to be the high point. In 1884 there were 19,406 lady associates, 71,181 members and 640 branches. These numbers had risen by 1892 to 28,907 associates, 132,084 members and 32,219 candidates. By 1914 there were 39,433 associates, 196,321 members and 83,684 candidates in the 1,749 branches organized in over 7,000 parishes in England and abroad.

The objective of this vast society was very largely to bring the working-class members under the supervision of the upper-class lady, in order to unite country girls coming to the city with the better aspects of urban living. Thus Lady Laura Ridding in the Church Congress of 1894 remarked that there were 'girls of fourteen living alone in lodgings'. These were often undesirable places. For recreation such a girl took to the 'gay streets and the riff-raff loiterers of a city crowd'. She received no training at all for marriage or motherhood. Lady Ridding appealed to the wives and daughters of factory owners to take a lead in providing a suitable 'woman superintendent' for such employees 'with . . . deputies' to look after their welfare and discipline.[35] Sometimes the GFS had very practical ends; in the *Guardian* of 27 July 1913 there is a report of a GFS Conference at which some of the subjects considered were 'homeless girls; sick members; registry; literature'.

[35] B. H. Harrison, 'For Church, Queen and Family: The Girls' Friendly Society, 1874–1920', *Past and Present*, 61 (1973), 107–38; CCR (1885), Townsend, p. 156; *Church of England Year-book* (1884), 76; (1892), 74; (1914), 72; CCR (1894), Lady Laura Ridding, pp. 258–60.

'One of the most important subjects discussed was how best to meet the needs of the thousands of educated workers and students (for the most part from country homes) whose lives in London and other large cities are beset with dangers begotten of loneliness and the entire absence of controlling restraint.' At that point, just before the beginning of the First World War, over 35,000 churches in the country marked the anniversary of the Society with special services, and the GFS had bought no less than fifty sites for churches in western Canada. The War provided new opportunities for the GFS, on 25 June 1915 the *Church Times* reported that 'some 1,500 associates, members, etc., were in France and Germany at the time, and the Societies' lodges in Paris and Frankfurt were real havens of refuge. In Berlin the names of over 940 G.F.S. members and others were entered in the club-room book as having come for advice and help.' Nor did the work of the Society come to an end with the death of its founder in 1918; the *Church Times* of 11 January 1924 reported that in a parish church near Bristol, for example, 'the school buildings have been entirely redecorated and painted, electric lights have been installed in them, an excellent piano provided. The G.F.S. Branch has been responsible to pay for it all. This is a splendid example of "Service not self" as a motto.' In the following year, the fiftieth anniversary celebrations of the GFS included a huge rally at the Albert Hall which 'could have been filled over and over again'. Subjects discussed at the conference included 'Development of the Adolescent Brain and Group Settlements in Western Australia'.[36]

The Girls' Friendly Society, extensive though it was, by no means exhausted the extent of the Church of England's interest in girls' clubs. In 1893 Maud Stanley wrote of eight types of girls' clubs with a religious element which the national Church undertook. The most important single society other than the GFS in the Church of England during this period, run by women themselves, was the Women's Help Society (WHS). The difference between the two societies was simply that the WHS did not require

[36] *Church Times*, 26 June 1925.

chastity for girls 'as a prerequisite for membership'. As the Revd Edmund Venables said in the Church Congress of 1885, the WHS was an intermediate group 'including such girls as work in mills. . . . Many mill-girls and others cannot, alas, be called actually pure, and yet they may not have fallen to the lowest depths and may be lifted.' The WHS was a parochial and diocesan society, usually under Anglo-Catholic auspices. By 1892 there were eighty-six branches in England, eight in Scotland, and one in Jamaica. The WHS always remained a dominantly male preserve as far as its government went. The London Diocesan Conference report of 1885 reveals a committee consisting entirely of men to deal with matters concerning 'the welfare of young women'. There is no doubt, according to the *Explanatory Pamphlet* of 1893, that the organization of the WHS was profoundly parochial, and that its object was to provide help to the parish priest. Also provided were two 'central homes' in London 'for the accommodation of ladies'. The WHS apparently went out of business when the GFS in 1936 renounced its purity rule.[37]

The work of individual Girls' Clubs must also be remembered. In the words of Charles Booth, these 'succeed wherever they are fairly tried, and must hold a very important place in the summary of the influences now at work upon character: especially in districts where the life of the streets is the only alternative'. Anglicans had taken a very large part in the foundation and the beginning of the YWCA. In 1918 Maude Royden observed that 'only the other day I read from some mournful priest of the Church of England that it looks as if in the future we shall have to choose between the Holy Catholic Church and the Holy Catholic Y.W.C.A. and I feel inclined to say that if this is so, it is the fault of the Church. Here are associations which have given to the people a scope for their work and service which the Church has not yet given.'[38]

[37] See Maud Stanley in Burdett-Coutts (ed.), *Woman's Mission*, pp. 49–50; Harrison, 'Girls' Friendly Society', p. 118; CCR (1885), Edmund Venables; CCR (1885), London Diocesan Conference; *Explanatory Pamphlet* (n.d. but received in the Bodleian Library, Oxford, 14 Nov. 1893); *Church Times*, 5 June 1936, 6 May 1921, 12 May 1922, 30 May 1924.

[38] Booth, *Religious Influences*, vii. 17; *Christian Commonwealth*, 27 Nov. 1918.

Not surprisingly the main pressure on women's work in the Church was on mothering, not only through the Mothers' Union, founded in 1887, but through individual mothers' meetings in parochial settings throughout the period. Although in the early years the interest of these was narrow and the education of the participants low, by 1929 both the interest and education of participants was high: one observer commented that 'all the women of a congregation are welcomed in these fellowships, as well as those outside. The fellowships are interested in questions of health, politics, local government, international questions, and overseas work; but the main object is to meet together for spiritual renewal, for prayer and praise, to learn more about God and the Christian faith and its implications for every-day life.'[39] The Mothers' Union became involved in various vocational enterprises, but its primary concern was always to further parenting. In the *Church Times* of 13 December 1912 for example, Mrs Sumner, the founder of the Mothers' Union, remarked that 'there were in the world two Divine institutions ordained by God himself—the Church and the home . . . The home was being undermined.' She was referring to the Divorce Bill proposed before the war, to which the Mothers' Union was always opposed. After the war, other people took up the cause of the family usually articulating their views through the Mothers' Union. In the mid-1920s the *Church Times* warned against allowing inadequate mothers into the Mothers' Union. 'The Union exists to commend a high ideal to Christian mothers and to defend the sanctity of marriage and it is of the first importance, therefore, that no natural desire for a large roll of members should lead to the inclusion of mothers who are, to say the least, imperfectly acquainted with the objects to which they are pledged.' The three main objects of the Mothers' Union were established in 1896 and reaffirmed in 1912 and 1926 when the constitution was revised: first, 'to uphold the sanctity of marriage'; second, 'to awaken in all mothers a sense of their responsibility in the training of their boys and girls'; and third, 'to organise every place a band of

[39] *Ranyard Magazine* (Jan. 1929), 3–4.

mothers who will unite in prayer and seek by their own example to lead their families in purity and holiness of life'. The first of these aims was interpreted very strictly throughout the history of the Mothers' Union—too strictly, in fact, for the bishops. The question of divorce had always been a difficult one for membership of the Union, and for the women's movement generally. None the less, 'the thing that is certain is that women will insist on being consulted, and that the attitude which the women of a country take up will mainly determine the solution reached'.[40]

Despite this particular problem, the growth of the Mothers' Union was phenomenal between 1910 and 1930. Starting in only one parish in the diocese of Winchester it spread throughout that diocese and elsewhere in England and overseas. By 1896 there were said to be 'nearly 100,000 members'. By 1900 the number had risen to about 157,000 members in over 3,370 branches and the *Journal* of the organization had up to 95,000 subscribers. In 1909 after twenty-two years' work there were about 300,000 members in parochial and diocesan organizations. On the eve of the First World War in 1913 the number had risen to 414,000, of which there were 350,000 in England; and by 1938 the *Church Times* claimed that there were over 600,000 members in 14,000 branches 'at home and overseas', with 457 delegates at the Annual General Conference. At that time the organization supported 'twenty workers in the mission field and maintained seven caravans, besides distributing generously to the missionary societies'.

Although the first purpose of the Mothers' Union was always motherhood and marriage it is true that it was viewed as 'the chief but not the sole or only profession of women'. The Revd Cyril Hepher, a missioner of Winchester, spoke to the annual diocesan service in 1914 of 'a halo . . . above the head of every true mother since Jesus was born of Mary' and went on to talk about the 'deliberate refusal of childbearing' as a good intention. Nevertheless, Mrs Creighton warned in the year after against undue pre-

---

[40] *Church Times*, 22 June 1923; *Workers' Papers*, Jan. 1923; *Church Times*, 27 June 1924, 29 Apr. 1927; *Newcastle Evening Chronicle*, 24 Mar. 1928; B. H. Streeter and Edith Picton-Turbervill, *Woman and the Church* (London, 1917), 17–19.

occupation with motherhood and stressed the need for individuality in each female person resident in the state. She wrote that 'parents were to send the girls as well as their boys out into the world to make a career: they must teach their children to discipline themselves; they were to see that their children were trained to serve the whole community of which their own family was but a unit, the most insidious form of selfishness being family selfishness'. From the very beginning, the Mothers' Union was enthusiastic about 'joint parenting', and the interest continued; there were some like Hensley Henson who argued for the sole vocation of motherhood for women, but many of the Mothers' Union's supporters favoured a wider sense of vocation.

The volunteer movement was by far the most important source of female action and activity within the Established Church in the late nineteenth century, and according to the *Church Times* the Mothers' Union had been far and away the most successful organization which had ever existed within the Anglican communion; and with the possible exception of the scouting movement, which was not specifically Christian in outlook, the story of its rise in the thirty years before the First World War 'can hardly be paralleled outside the pages of the Acts of the Apostles'. Without a doubt the Mothers' Union was the most important volunteer organization within the Church of England in the late Victorian and Edwardian periods. Yet, as we shall see, it was not the only form of women's participation in church work during that time.[41]

[41] Bishops' Meeting, fo. 100, Lambeth, 26 May 1925; *Church Times*, 6 June 1913, 22 June 1923; *Church of England Year-book* (1913), 66, 72; CCR (1909), Lady Acland, p. 482; *Church Times*, 6 June 1913, 3 June 1938; Charles Raven, *Women and Holy Orders* (London, 1928), 22; *Church Times*, 3 Apr. 1914, 18 June 1915. See also *Newcastle Evening Chronicle*, 24 Mar. 1928; *Church Times*, 22 June 1928.

3

Paid and Professed Workers

CHURCH work by women was primarily philanthropic in the late-Victorian years, but it was not confined to the activity of volunteers. Among other forms of pre-professional work open to women was that of the paid parish visitor. Comparatively few in number and of very humble social rank, their duty was to make contact with the 'class of persons below the decent poor',[1] to evangelize those whom the church notoriously failed to reach, and to assist them towards domestic self-help as well as salvation.

The heroine and founder of the biblewomen's movement was Ellen Henrietta Ranyard (1810–79), wife of Benjamin Ranyard, a philanthropist. In her mid-teen years she had distributed bibles among the poor and she was closely associated with the Bible Society for most of her life. In 1853 she wrote for that society *The Book and its Story*, which was a considerable popular success. Four years later she took her first walk through a real London slum, Seven Dials in St Giles, and there faced the problem, 'how to get the Bible effectively to these people?' Contact with the local clergy made it clear that bibles could be made available. But how, she wondered, could one get the very poor to buy?

She came into contact with a poor woman of St Giles known thereafter as 'Marian B.', who had been given a bible while in hospital a few years before. 'Marian B.' recalled,

During the time I was in hospital I had frequent opportunity of witnessing the utterly friendless condition of many poor outcasts who sought admission to its charity, the filthy plight of their persons and clothing proving their need of a female hand to rectify disorder . . . how I would wish to dedicate the time I

[1] L. N. R[anyard], *The Missing Link: or Bible-Women in the Homes of the London Poor* (London, 1859), 31.

have to spare (it might be two or three hours a day), not so much to the decent poor . . . but to the lost and degraded of my own sex, whom from their vicious lives, no tenderly reared female would be likely to approach; but to me, who, by God's mercy, was preserved in my youth from a like fate, such scenes will have no terror . . . It will be enough for her to require my aid—such as cleansing and washing and repairing her garments.[2]

With Mrs Ranyard and 'Marian B.' the two essential human elements in the plan came together: the lady super-intendent and the humble worker. Biblewomen came from the poorer classes themselves; their mission was to the even poorer. From the beginning the scheme had a double thrust: on the one hand its principal object was to sell cheap bibles and testaments among the poor; in addition it aimed to improve the physical and moral situation of the depressed classes of women and their families by such self-help and mutually supportive associations as clothing and bedding clubs and mothers' meetings, and to provide individual help and companionship when called upon. Before long, the movement had spread through several London districts including Paddington, Clerkenwell, Spitalfields, Bethnal Green, and Shoreditch.[3]

The biblewomen's second task unquestionably con-tained a measure of social control. In her book *The Missing Link*, Mrs Ranyard wrote that the provision of soup and the encouragement of saving for bedding were designed to divert money and interest from strong drink. 'Marian B.' was convinced that 'a clean, kind, sober woman almost always makes a good husband'. On the other hand if a wife 'sits about dirty and idle and never has a clean hearth or a nice cup of tea for him when he comes in from his work, [she] need not wonder if he goes to the public house and spends there in one night what would keep the family for a week'.[4] The biblewomen's movement was not a Church initiative, and it remained unsectarian through the twentieth century. However, it received substantial

---

[2] Ibid., 13–14. See also Lizzie Aldridge, *The World's Workers* (London, 1885), *passim*.

[3] R[anyard], *The Missing Link*, pp. 47–51, 116, 124, 161.

[4] Ibid., 35.

Anglican support, while 'Free Church support seemed to tail off considerably, especially in the 1920s.[5]

What did the biblewoman's movement amount to? Leaving aside the distinct nursing division, which began in 1868 and undoubtedly transformed the overall shape of the Ranyard Mission, it involved evangelistic and social service work by paid women, very many of whom were associated with the Established Church. The number of biblewomen connected with the Ranyard Mission in London in 1858 was about seven; it rapidly (and yearly) rose to 234 by 1867. In those same years (1858–67) receipts from all sources (including payments by the poor for bibles and other articles as well as substantial donations) amounted to £133,377—by no means an insignificant sum. In this early period the salary of a biblewoman seems to have been ten shillings a week for a five-day week of five hours per day, although by 1894 this rose to 12s. 6d.[6]

It was a basic principle of the London Female Bible and Domestic Mission (the formal name for Mrs Ranyard's creation) that its agents must be poor women who were paid for their work, while the general rules of the organization provided that 'each Bible woman shall be placed under the careful superintendence of a Lady who may be found willing to undertake the work and who is a resident in the District, or within a reasonable distance from it'. This lady was to receive a weekly report from her charge, pay the biblewoman's salary, and 'give such directions as the local circumstances may require'. These lady superintendents (part of the volunteer army which was the subject of Chapter 2) numbered 143 in 1874.[7] They were apparently independent of male ecclesiastical or other control in their disposition of funds: 'to each of the Lady Superintendents has been committed the expenditure of money allotted to each district for . . . the biblewoman's *salary*, the *rent* of her mission-room and the *incidental*

---

[5] *Ranyard Magazine* (Apr. 1930), 24.

[6] L. N. R[anyard], *London and Ten Years' Work in It* (London, 1868), 8; 10; R[anyard], *The Missing Link*, p. 292; Booth, *Life and Labour of the People of London*, (3rd edn.) (London, 1896), 196.

[7] R[anyard], *The Missing Link*, p. 291; L. N. R[anyard], *Nurses for the Needy* (London, 1875), 223.

expenses of light, fire and cleaning, together with the provision of material for a Clothing Club'.[8]

A very significant addition to her mission was made by Mrs Ranyard in 1868 with the establishment of a nurses' division. Such a nurse was 'often drawn from mothers' classes', and in addition to possessing appropriate maternal qualities was to be 'a godly woman unencumbered if possible with family cares of her own and yet having a motherly and missionary heart'. These women would have the customary three-month training as biblewomen together with another hospital stint of three months and additional experience in a lying-in institution. They would have the benefit of supervision by lady superintendents and the advantage of a central 'mother-house' to provide for their 'needful supplies and directions while they themselves live out in the world's great hospital'.[9]

After Mrs Ranyard's death in 1879, and particularly in the early years of this century, the mission developed in three ways. First, the two parts diverged, becoming more definitely separate in training and function, and the nursing side began to dominate. Second, the mission became predominantly Anglican, destined to merge with the developing general parish work for women in the period after the First World War. Third, the independence which Mrs Ranyard and her lady superintendents had enjoyed seemed largely to vanish as parish priests obtained clear supervisory powers, and bishops and other clergymen appeared on the Ranyard Council.

In the 1890s, as part of a general interest in training and expertise, the training of biblewomen was greatly improved. A hostel 'for the reception and training of mission candidates' was opened in which 'systematic Bible teaching' was supplemented by 'lectures on Hygiene and on Organised Methods of Relief', and a three-month stay was required (it rose to six months by 1919). This work was transferred to Ranyard House by 1907. In addition to the theorists of the Bible and Charity Organisation Societies, and to knowledge of the Prayer Book and training in

---

8 R[anyard], *London and Ten Years' Work in It*, pp. 11–12.
9 R[anyard], *Nurses for the Needy*, pp. 35, 41, 464.

Sunday School, there should also be 'insights into the working of girls' clubs, girl guides, training for the conduct of women's meetings and in all parochial and district work'. In 1916 28 Ranyard workers were labouring heroically in the London diocese and each received a certificate in recognition from the Bishop of London.[10] The *Official Year-book of the Church of England* indicates that the total number of twentieth-century Bible mission women never reached the nineteenth-century upper level. Rising from 84 in 1906 to 110 in the first year of the World War there was regular decline thereafter to 64 in 1926, and 60 in 1930.

At the annual meeting of the Ranyard Mission in 1917 (the name changed from the London Bible Women and Nurses Mission to the Ranyard Mission: Mission Women and District Nurses), Canon Gedge, a member of the council of the Mission, spoke of the support a biblewoman received from her training in Ranyard House. He also drew attention to 'that system which this society employs of sending down picked women—picked spiritually and mentally—to strengthen that solitary woman. Oh! The bright look when that visit has been paid, when the Superintendent . . . has been round.' This is the last known mention of the lady superintendent system. More and more emphasis was placed on the biblewoman as an integral part of the parish or congregational structure. Indeed, the non-Anglican side seems to have rapidly declined. In 1923, only ten of seventy biblewomen were Free Church agents and the following appeared in the *Ranyard Magazine:*

The small Free Churches in poor areas cannot afford even part of the salary of a woman worker and the higher churches wish for the help of women of higher education who take a two or three years' course at one of the various denominational training centres. . . . We have not dared to take in more than one [Free Church] candidate at a time for years past: and now it is only possible to take one if she is willing to train on the understanding that at the end of six months we may not be able to place her.

10 *Ranyard Magazine* (Apr. 1917), 90; (Jan. 1919), 16.

On the other hand, Anglican demand outran supply. By 1917, the year of the Mission's jubilee, the Ranyard's council contained five bishops, a good many other clergymen, and Mrs Randall Davidson, the wife of the archbishop of Canterbury.[11] More and more the Ranyard Mission, on its evangelistic side, looked like a source of female pastoral aid to the Church of England, and seemed much less independent of the Establishment's organization and function than its original form suggested. Meanwhile biblewomen's pay rose modestly. A report in the *Guardian* on 14 March 1918 pointed out that members of a Liverpool branch of the organization got up to £1 per week. By the end of the 1920s, the salary of mission women generally was £115 p.a. plus pension and uniform.[12]

As the Bible mission women tended to merge with Church organizations, so the nurses' division generally went its own professional way, increasingly detached from the evangelistic stem. Although the *Ranyard Magazine* insisted that 'bearing witness to Our Lord is unalterable as the one great theme of Mission' in June 1917, the same article noted significant changes in the training and supervision of nurses. 'The Mission must be linked up with hospitals and other public services in order to ensure the most fruitful and economic results.' From June 1899 nurses were officially involved in the care of schoolchildren, properly attached to hospitals with respect to maternity care, and doing systematic and medically-supervised work in connection with out-patient departments of hospitals. Indeed the Ranyard nurses became a recognized and integral part of the nursing system of London, a status confirmed by membership in the Central Council of District Nursing in 1913. Unlike the case of the evangelistic mission branch, the early twentieth century was a period of modest growth for the nurses' branch. Starting with about fourteen in 1868, the number of nurses rose steadily from the end of the First World War through the 1920s. There were seventy-nine Ranyard nurses functioning in

1918 and ninety-five in 1929. The 1930s brought a slight
increase in numbers. The principal training emphasis was
on the need for 'fully trained' nurses, although there was
still a three-week probationary period required to assess a
candidate's capacity to deal with the 'expressed spiritual
needs of patients'. The nurse's training at Ranyard House,
in hospital, and under a 'superintending sister' in an
assigned district, was definitely medical. It is clear that
there was still an element of Christian connection; but the
Ranyard nurses, by the late 1920s, were nurses first and
foremost. [13]

Whereas Mrs Ranyard deliberately established a non-
denominational mission, which veered towards ancillary
status in the Church of England only long after her death,
her contemporary, Caroline Jane Talbot (1809–76)
intended her parochial mission women to be female agents
of the Church system from their foundation in 1860. Mrs
Talbot (wife of J. C. Talbot, who died in 1852) was much
influenced by the Oxford Movement; she was a friend of
Mrs Gladstone, and mother of E. S. Talbot, first Warden of
Keble College, who was married to Mrs Gladstone's niece.
She was a type of Victorian lady who dominated despite
her sex, no doubt partly because of her social position as
the granddaughter of a duke. Her son and biographer
wrote, 'entire absence of feminine weakness and wonderful intensity and constancy of maternal affection [marked
her] . . . But her strengths did not unsex her . . . No lack
of womanly refinement [was evident].' Although, he went
on, 'men who spoke to her spoke direct to her understanding' and she wrote 'in a man's style rather than a
woman's', yet he insisted that 'she preserved womanly
modesty and showed no ambition to thrust herself
forward or to claim for her sex unusual functions'. [14]

Mrs Talbot evidently picked up the idea of parochial
mission women from a letter in the *Guardian* of 4 July 1860
in which the writer pointed to the need for biblewomen

[13] *Ranyard Magazine* (June 1917), 148–9. Numbers appear in Annual Reports,
which always appear in the April issues of the *Ranyard Magazine*. Ibid. (July
1928), 67–9.
[14] John G. Talbot (ed.), *Memorials of the Hon. Mrs. John Chetwynd Talbot*
(London, 1876), 13.

who were attached firmly to the parish structure of the Church. Shortly thereafter some six women were at work, and a new organization for the employment of poor women under church auspices was launched. In the early 1860s a good deal of attention was given to this new organization in the *Guardian* and in the meetings of the new Church Congress. For example, at the 1862 Congress, the Revd C. Wellington Furse gave a summary of its principles. Above all, 'the mission should in all things be subordinate to the parochial system'. That of course, meant subordinate to the parish priest, who must initiate the request for a worker, choose the individual, and select a lady superintendent under whose immediate direction she should work. Secondly, the 'mission woman is taken from the ranks of the poor'. The point here was exactly as with the biblewomen, except that in this context comparison was made with other Church workers: 'a door has been opened to the poor, through which we have hitherto seen only sisters of gentler blood . . . pass within the veil of a devoted life'. Thirdly, these women aimed to develop self-help among the poor; they were not to distribute alms but to collect pennies to allow 'for the purchase by instalment of Bibles and Prayer-Books, articles of clothing and bedding'. Only soup was actually given, and then only to the sick. A single mission was constituted by one mission woman and one lady superintendent in a single parish. It was usual to have a weekly meeting (of between twelve and forty) with the mission woman and the superintendent, the purpose of which was to settle accounts, to dispense and receive advice, to read and listen to readings. It was said that twenty-eight parishes had such missions by 1862 and that a single mission cost about £32 a year.[15]

As was the case with biblewomen, the numbers of parochial mission women grew rapidly in the last quarter of the nineteenth century, as the work begun in London spread elsewhere. By 1884 there were 187 parochial church mission women and in the late 1880s the numbers rose to

---

[15] CCR (1862), 135–9; A Lady Manager, *A Servant of the Poor: or Some Account of the Life and Death of a Parochial Mission-Woman* (London, 1874), 36; see also *Guardian*, 23 July 1862.

over 200, something never again achieved after 1890 although the *Official Year-book of the Church of England* continued to list the organization until 1922 when there were about 38 active agents left, nearly all in the dioceses of London and Southwark. Annual collections, which amounted to £217,000 in the first twenty-three years reached a peak, apparently, in 1886 when £115,000 was collected in very small sums for the various saving projects.[16] Charles Booth praised, in orthodox Charity Organisation Society fashion, the value of this technique.

It is found in practice that unless they collect, those who visit the poor can hardly avoid giving: but if collecting is their business they may go to the very same house without being expected to give . . . [It results in] placing visitation on a business footing . . . To make the visit acceptable class superiority is no longer necessary; all trace of patronage vanishes, and if any remains it is the depositor who becomes the patron and would receive the acknowledgement of thanks . . . No social development of the day seems to me more promising than this of the organised collection of savings by those who seek with single minds the . . . welfare of people.[17]

There is no doubt that the parochial mission woman, unlike the original biblewoman, was deliberately placed to strengthen the parish system itself. Canon Liddon believed such mission women, because of their humble status, could gain 'admission to thousands of homes from which a Sister of Mercy would be excluded'. Once in the home, the mission woman would work in all sorts of ways to prepare the way for and supplement the work of the incumbent: 'to report and to relieve distress; to nurse sickness; to give elementary instruction; to help persons prepare for baptism or communion; to establish and deepen relations of confidence between the people and their parish priest'. As was the case with the biblewoman, so too the parochial mission woman had secular uses. She was, in Liddon's words, 'a servant of the nation', and it was her task to 'heal any of our social sores', to prevent

[16] *Church of England Year-books* are the source of most stations; CCR (1883), 149.
[17] Booth, *Religious Influences*, vii. 21–2.

social and political tensions and disruptions, and 'to strengthen the enfeebled forces of religion,—the only real guarantee in the long run of social or of national safety'.[18]

It is clear that by the 1880s both biblewomen and parochial mission women were offering paid work for women within the accepted religious framework. Each of their organizations had over 200 women at work in London selling bibles, establishing soup kitchens and clothing clubs, organizing mothers' meetings, and extending the pastoral ministry of the parish clergy. From the 1890s it is apparent that the fortunes of the biblewomen and those of the parochial mission women diverged significantly; whereas the mission women declined in numbers, the Ranyard organization continued to thrive well into the twentieth century. Two factors seemed to account for this difference. Firstly, the Ranyard mission developed a nursing side from 1868 which became a significant factor in London district nursing; secondly, whereas the parochial mission women seemed never to have developed a training scheme, the Ranyard mission did so from 1895. As in the case of voluntary district nurses it was becoming clear that the way of the future for paid church workers was that of expertise and clear standards. The prize of survival went to those who recognized the new passion for training.

Another organization which developed women's church work according to the customs of an age of subordination was the Church Army. Founded by Prebendary Wilson Carlile in 1883 as an Anglican imitation of the Salvation Army, it developed a separate women's branch in 1887. These women were expected to 'nurse, visit, take classes and mothers' meetings [and] assist at Church Army meetings'. Although they were not identified as officer-evangelists, and their ministry was clearly supplemental to that of Church Army officers (in this respect the situation was markedly different from that of Salvation Army women), there was some fear, voiced especially by Hensley Henson, about the possibility of their preaching in public. An official statement was issued which placed the labours of these women strictly in the context of

[18] H. P. Liddon, *Phoebe in London*, pp. 20–1.

subordination. 'Headquarters feel that the post of Captain [the common rank of Church Army male officers] is not in any way suitable for women, whose duty is not so much the terrible anxiety of leading, as to do all they can to win souls in submission to another's authority.' In January 1887 a ten-week course of training was begun for Church Army sisters marked by evangelistic work, a 'good ambulance course', and 'hospital experience'. Two years later it was taken over by Marie Carlile, sister of the Army's founder. The first candidates were from 'the reservoir of unmarried middle-class "ladies"', but by the end of the 1880s most were domestic servants and shop workers. By 1895, of the thirty-four candidates accepted for training, there were seventeen domestic servants, three shop workers, three nurses, two missionaries of other sorts, a dressmaker, a weaver, a porter, a warehouse girl, a 'companion', and only four designated 'ladies'. This social shape generally persisted. Numerically the Church Army became the most significant source of female proletarian Church workers. From 192 'mission nurses' (plus 18 described as 'associate mission nurses') in 1900, the numbers rose steadily to 429 by 1913. As early as 1907, it seems that 400 had been reached. The total number trained over the years to 1937 was 2,000.[19]

The work of the Church Army mission sisters was varied, much of it comparable to that of parochial mission women. Certainly many were directly attached to parishes. One clergyman wrote to the *Guardian* (24 August 1904) about parish-based Church Army sisters in a new London working-class suburb of 5,000 people. As the priest in charge, he rented a cottage for 5s. 6d. a week and installed two Church Army women at a salary of 16s. a week apiece. He went on to describe how they operated.

The women are trained workers and visited regularly from house to house among the people. Twice each week they

---

[19] Graham Simpson, 'A Sociological Study of the Church Army: The Origins and Development of a Church of England Society', D. Phil. thesis (Oxford, 1979), 299–301 and 357–8. The quotation within Simpson is from the *Church Army Gazette* (1887), 144; A. E. Reffold, *A Noble Army of Women; Marie Carlile and the Church Army Sisters* (London, 1947), 11.

brought me a detailed list of these visits, with remarks upon all cases calling for special attention . . . severe sickness, need of relief, children unbaptised or not attending Sunday-school, young people of an age for Confirmation, etc. Thus a conspectus of the whole population, kept up-to-date, was always in my hands.[20]

They conducted meetings of fifteen to twenty regularly in the front room of the cottage, and taught volunteers how to help in parish work. And, of course, their service had a secular side: 'they had at least an elementary knowledge of sick-nursing: they knew how to report a case to the medical officer of health or to the sanitary inspector and they knew when to call the Society for the Prevention of Cruelty to Children'. All this was obtained for not more than £100 a year, including the cottage.

Church Army women, however, did other things as well, some of a less conventional sort. We are told they undertook 'sea-side missions' in such places as Weymouth and Ramsgate, visits to women's prisons from 1895, a mission to barmaids, rescue work, and some medical mission activity.[21] It was, perhaps, some suspicion of this extra-parochial initiative which prevented the bishops from agreeing to the request that Church Army mission women should have official Church recognition in 1907. A committee of the Upper House of Canterbury Convocation considered a request which would have granted an official status parallel (but not the same) as that given to Church Army male evangelists (who were considered lay readers). The Upper House committee refused official recognition on the ground that other groups (such as parochial mission women) would have equal claims. The Convocation committee pointed out that the only women workers regularly set apart (by) the laying-on of hands were deaconesses, and that Church Army women were by no means the same. On the other hand, on 30 April 1907 the following motion was carried by the Upper House: 'that heartily appreciating the excellent work done by the Church Army mission women, while of opinion it would not be expedient

[20] Reffold, *A Noble Army of Women*, p. 22.
[21] Ibid., pp. 29, 35.

to give any such recognition to them as the adoption of a form of licence would imply, we commend them to the sympathetic encouragement of the bishops in their several dioceses'. This vague authorization was all they received until they (like the Church Army men) were admitted as Lay Evangelists. In the meantime, Wilson Carlile himself described the Church Army women (*Guardian*, 30 July 1914) as 'humble-minded keen women' given scope to 'preach the gospel', who considered their 'province [to be] . . . that of the evangelistic prophetess living . . . for the poorest of the land'. At the same time he emphatically denied any desire of Church Army women to be priests, 'any such idea would be entirely repugnant to them'.[22]

The presence of several hundred biblewomen, parochial mission women, and Church Army mission women in the last decades of the Victorian era and in the first years of the twentieth century shows that it was possible for humble single women to engage in 'church work' for pay, even in 'the age of subordination'. The Church did its best to contain such work within the arena of extended domesticity, confining women's evangelistic efforts to other women, and maintaining the ultimate authority of men (as parish priests and bishops). Biblewomen, who began free of parochial limitations, obviously found such attachments more useful than inhibiting in the twentieth century. In all these cases the Church clearly showed its reluctance to license, or officially to sanction in any way, any special style of women's work within the institution.

One sector of Church work which admitted hundreds of largely middle-class single women for paid employment in the late nineteenth century was the foreign mission field. In the twentieth century the conduct and administration of missions, both at home and at stations abroad, became a matter of concern to the women's movement. In the previous century women's work in foreign missions fitted the ideology of subordination, although it also revealed defects in that ideology as a guide to sexual roles.

[22] Chronicles of Convocation (Canterbury) (hereafter cited as CC), 30 April 1907, p. 74. See also Report 411, Upper House Committee; Reffold, *A Noble Army of Women*, p. 20.

Of the two large and established Anglican missionary societies, the Society for the Propagation of the Gospel (SPG) and the Church Missionary Society (CMS), the SPG being more firmly tied to the ecclesiastical structure and to the Church's catholic tradition, was less inclined to accept independent women missionaries. In 1842, for example, a woman offered herself for service to the bishop of Calcutta and was refused as follows: 'I object on principle to single ladies coming out unprotected to so distant a place with a climate so unfriendly and the almost certainty of their marrying within a month of their arrival.' He went on to express his belief that holy ladies of old 'who laboured much in the Lord, remained in their own neighbourhoods and families, and that no unmarried female would have thought of a voyage of 14,000 miles to find out a scene of duty. The whole thing is against the Apostolic maxim "I suffer not a woman to speak in the Church".' In 1867 an SPG single woman missionary was assigned to Madagascar, although because of delays in Mauritius she did not reach her destination until 1874. There does not seem any real sign of further SPG initiatives in this respect until the twentieth century, although some serious training for women missionaries was begun in the 1890s.[23]

The Church Missionary Society was quicker to recognize the value of the single female missionary and to make her a significant agent in the foreign field. As early as 1815, several women offered to work among those Hindu women in India who were kept in seclusion and were inaccessible therefore to male missionary enterprise. They were turned down on traditional grounds: 'the committee [of the CMS] after discussion . . . resolved not to send unmarried women abroad except sisters accompanying or joining their brothers'. The committee evidently relented to the extent of sending two such ladies to Sierra Leone in 1819, although one apparently went to accompany her brother.[24] There was very little change in this attitude until the 1880s.

The lever which opened up the mission field to independent women was, in fact, the very instrument which was

[23] Humphry, *Ministries of Women During Fifty Years with the S.P.G.*, pp. 8–9, 13–14, 18.
[24] Stock, *The History of The CMS*, i. 125.

proposed to the CMS committee and rejected in 1815. This was that, in the words of a lady in 1900, 'only women missionaries can gain entrance to the Zenanas of India, where millions of *purdah* women spend their lives. With childish, untaught minds they are quite unfit to be companions for educated husbands'. Similarly, it was argued that in 'all the lands where Islam holds sway . . . if the women are to be reached it must be done by women'.[25] This was an irresistible argument; not only did the conversion of this class of females depend on the evangelistic powers of women Christians, but, unless it were achieved, the whole of Indian domestic life (that sphere for which women were uniquely responsible) would remain unchristianized, and the raising of Indian children would inevitably remain heathen.

At first the CMS was prepared to sponsor such work only if it were undertaken by 'their missionaries' wives, widows and the female members of the Mission families'. However, in mid-century an independent society under female control, the Indian Female Normal School and Instruction Society, was founded precisely for that task. It was later to be re-named the Zenana Bible and Medical Mission. In 1880 a number of Church of England women established the Church of England Zenana Missionary Society with thirty-two missionaries on its role and several stations in north and south India. It was still functioning in the 1930s.[26]

The last two decades of the nineteenth century saw a marked change in the CMS attitude to women missionaries. In 1887 the number on the staff was only twenty-two. However, in that year alone seventeen were added (in China, Africa, Palestine, and Japan) and between 1887 and 1894 no less than 214 women (not including wives) came on to the CMS roll.[27] Much of this change of heart was due to the Society's secretary Eugene

---

[25] National Union of Women Workers, *The Papers Read at the Conference Held at Brighton on October 23, 24, 25, and 26, 1900* (London, 1900), 26-7.

[26] Stock, *The History of the CMS*, ii. 399. See also A. M. Robinson, *Women to Women: the Work of the C.E.M.S.*, reprinted from *The East and West Review* [1935], *passim*.

[27] Stock, *The History of the CMS*, ii. 399; iii. 369.

Stock, described by his biographer as a keen advocate of women in the mission field, and, to a woman, Miss G. A. Gollock, whom Stock appointed in 1890 as his assistant. In 1895 Miss Gollock was appointed 'Lady Secretary' of a new 'Women's Department' of the CMS to supervise not only the training and assignment of the increasing number of female missionaries, but to provide 'friends and counsellors of their own sex at headquarters, not only before they go out and when on furlough, but while at work in the field'. The vocation of the single woman missionary was clearly being recognized, whatever her particular skill or technical qualification, whether medical, literary and educational, evangelistic, or pastoral. The International Congress of Women put out a report on 'Professions open to Women' in 1899 which noted that 'the mission field in India, China, Africa, and Armenia now presents a great opening to women whose sympathy and zeal dispose them to cooperate with the twenty-seven foreign missionary societies [of various denominations] now availing themselves of their services'.[28]

Meanwhile Miss Gollock at the CMS was concerning herself with the screening, training, and equipment of women preparing to go overseas. No matter what their specialist qualifications, she insisted that only 'spiritual . . . women are needed for spiritual work', that 'all training should be probationary', and that the personal selection of candidates was very important. Thus, at the end of the century, all candidates were sent for a period (which varied up to two years) to one of several 'training homes' some run by deaconesses. There they studied the Bible, Christian doctrine, and the Book of Common Prayer as well as domestic matters, nursing, simple surgery, and district visiting. They also considered the conduct of mothers' meetings and Sunday school work. In addition they were examined as to their 'devotion to Christ and subjection to the Holy Spirit', 'loyal attachment to . . .

[28] Georgina Gollock, *Eugene Stock: A Biographical Study, 1836 to 1948* (London, 1929), 170–3; Eugene Stock, *My Recollections* (London, 1909), 157–8; Stock, *The History of the CMS*, iii. 663, 694; A. E. Ball, 'The Need and Scope of Women's Work', *Church Missionary Intelligencer*, 20 NS (1895), 42–3; The Countess of Aberdeen (ed.), *The International Congress of Women, 1899* (London, 1899), 32.

Church principles', their 'proved capacity to work well with others' and their possession of 'a temperament sound and free from morbid tendencies'. Three initial references were required of each candidate and throughout a very careful check was made of her progress. The individual candidate was invited for interview by a committee of six (three clergy and three ladies) each of whom was given 'opportunity for a long close talk, closing with prayer' so that six interviews really resulted, every one issuing in a 'more or less detailed report'. By 1898, when this statement of practice was made, there were 253 women missionaries under the direction of the CMS. By 1905 the number of women equalled the number of clergy missionaries at 410, and in 1915 the women (at 444) were 30 more than the number of ordained men.[29]

Despite the development and considerable growth of work for single women in the mission field by the Edwardian years and the inevitable importance such work had for the expansion of the Church, their position of sub-ordination was little changed in any fundamental way. With the exception of the Zenana Mission (as we have seen, a peculiar case) women possessed little or no control or direction over policy matters either at home or abroad. It was also true that women were beginning to do things abroad (for example, lead in worship in the absence of a priest or other man) which were unthinkable at home. Yet as one speaker said of her experience in Indian missions in 1923, 'the doctrine of the subordination of woman to man had done a great deal of evil in the world and had been responsible for keeping back women missionaries and thereby retarding the spread of Christianity'.[30] It was part of the women's movement at home to gain the power and position in the great societies which their growing responsibility abroad justified.

[29] Georgina Gollock, 'The Training of Women Missionaries', *Church Missionary Intelligencer*, 23 NS, (1898), 39–43; Stock, *The History of the CMS*, iii. 704; iv. 465.

[30] M. C. Gollock, 'Women in the Church on the Mission Fields', in C. C. B. Bardsley (ed.), *Women and Church Work* (London, 1917), 72, 88; *Sheffield Daily Telegraph*, 9 March 1923.

The foreign mission field, unlike the home mission field, was a source of employment for Victorian middle-class women, 'the surplus spinster society'.[31] Numerically far more significant than missions in this respect (although not a paid employment in the direct sense) were sisterhoods. The revival of the religious life in the 1840s within the Church of England was a product of the Oxford Movement, an element in the growth of Catholic spirituality and devotion which helped stimulate the inner life of the Victorian Church. Despite a good deal of rabid Protestant prejudice, the movement grew rapidly, particularly amongst women. By 1875, there were eighteen sisterhoods in no less than ninety-five centres. They were responsible for a great deal of work. In that year Father T. T. Carter reported to the Church Congress that, on the medical side, over 1,000 'sick and helpless' were in their care, three large London hospitals were staffed entirely by sisters, hundreds of people were nursed annually in their homes by sisters, and many potential nurses were being trained. In penitentiary work (one of the original undertakings of the early Anglican orders) over 1,000 ex-prostitutes passed through the sisters' care. Some 6,000 children were 'under regular teaching' by the sisters, and other good works such as retreats, spiritual counselling, and foreign mission work had developed apace. Ten years later 'more than 1,300 sisters, with at least as many associates' were functioning in 'about thirty sisterhoods, some of these working at a dozen or even twenty separate centres'. This expansion evidently continued, so that by the 1920s Mrs Paget could say of the religious life that 'of all whole-time groups' [in which women worked for the Church] . . . [it was] the most attractive to women, although . . . least encouraged by authority'. In 1930, the prioress of Whitby, a speaker at the Anglo-Catholic Congress, was able to tell her audience that 'there are

---

[31] See Sarah Caroline Potter, 'The Social Origins and Recruitment of English Protestant Missionaries in the Nineteenth Century', Ph.D. thesis (London, 1974). This work contains a table showing the occupational backgrounds of female Victorian missionaries in various societies and denominations.

more women religious now in England than there were at the Reformation'.[32]

This was a far greater expansion than was experienced by other forms of mid-Victorian full-time women's church work. As the number and range of their undertakings in the 1870s shows, in most cases the *active work* of these ladies corresponded to labours often undertaken by others who were not dressed in special habits nor subject to the religious vows of poverty, obedience, and chastity, but who were paid in cash rather than provided with a living in kind and residence in community. Sisters were seen, of course, as a partial solution to the problem of the unattached (and unsupported) middle-class female, and even as a means of capturing for the Church energy which contemporary custom too often shut off from fruitful use. 'Few will now deny', stated a leading article in the *Guardian* of 31 March 1858, 'that there are as many capable and active-minded women as men in our upper and middle classes, yet how many fields are open to the one set, how few to the other.' The writer was moved to conclude with an uncharacteristically radical statement, 'it can never be right, in a complicated state of civilisation like ours, that domestic occupations should swallow up a whole female world'. There was some complaint that the early Victorian sisterhoods were socially too elevated; the point made was that 'it is a very great mistake to think that it requires either a high order of intellect or a superior education to attain to the devotion and self-abnegation of the Sister of Charity'.[33]

One distinctive feature of the religious life was (and is) its primary character as a life of prayer rather than as a vocation to pastoral or professional work. The self-giving, the oblation of the sister to Christ in community, was itself her prime work, expressed in the continual round of devotion required by the particular order's rule. In so far

[32] See A. M. Allchin, *The Silent Rebellion* (London, 1958), *passim*; CCR (1875), 52–3; (1885), 144; (1921), 231; *Report of the Anglo-Catholic Congress* (London, 1930), 192.

[33] *Women and Their Work*, reprinted from *The Ecclesiastic for January, 1855* (London, 1855), 20.

as the community was world-directed as well as God-centred (and the orders differed in the degrees as well as the types of active work undertaken), this thrust would first be shown by intercessory prayer. Communities of the Religious saw themselves 'as reservoirs of stored and strong devotion'. This God-centred style of life was a 'permanent state', a 'life of union with Christ'.[34]

From this unique base, members of religious communities no doubt undertook a wide variety of charitable good works under Church auspices in Victorian times and afterwards. In his 1908 Pan-Anglican Congress paper on the subject of such committees, Father Congreve of the Society of St John the Evangelist noted that sisters were 'pioneers in the adventure of rescuing fallen women in great cities and leading them through years of tender and firm discipline back to penitence and Christian life'. They provided, administered, and staffed schools of all sorts, from orphanages to high-schools for upper-class girls. They worked with the National Society for the Prevention of Cruelty to Children to rescue little girls. They worked in foreign missions. Perhaps their most striking 'secular' achievement was in nursing and in hospital work generally. Florence Nightingale, who had looked to German Lutherans for models of nursing practice, in fact used Anglican sisters as nurses in the Crimea. Although Miss Nightingale was clearly unhappy about religious sisterhoods as the basis for nursing, and sought instead a professional ethos with less emphasis on religious vocation and self-sacrifice, the religious orders certainly did make a substantial contribution to the development of the professional nurse in the period just before that profession developed. By Edwardian times, sisters were managing public hospitals in London, Calcutta, Bombay, and Cape Town, and provided and managed homes for the aged and hospitals for the dying.[35]

Much more was done by nurses within the plan of the parochial system, especially in home mission work,

[34] G. Congreve, 'Sisters: Their Vocation and Their Special Work' in *Pan-Anglican Papers* (London, 1908), 5; Allchin, *The Silent Rebellion*, pp. 141, 155.
[35] Congreve, 'Sisters', p. 5; Michael Hill, *The Religious Order* (London, 1973), 292; Congreve, 'Sisters', p. 7.

district visiting, and similar activity. Naturally Anglo-Catholic parishes were the most welcoming of such auxiliary help. Thus the Revd Bryan King testified before a parliamentary committee in the 1850s to the value of his Sisters in the St George's-in-the-East mission. They apparently lived within the parish where they operated a refuge for prostitutes; they also acted as district visitors and 'they nurse the people during sickness, and take charge of their children in the schools, and that opens the way to the clergy'. Church Congress speakers gave evidence in the 1870s of the superior quality of sisters' parish work, marked as it was by unusual self-sacrifice, devotion, and continuity. It was work which attracted the approval of that defender of subordination and devotee of domesticity J. W. Burgon.

All honour to those pious women who . . . devote themselves to the training of Christ's little ones—or to the nursing of the sick—or to the clothing of the naked—or to the visiting of the poor and outcast . . . these are 'home duties' every one . . . These holy women . . . carry their home virtues, their home graces, with them wherever they go . . . Who are the 'keepers of the home' if not *they* who, courting no publicity, attracting no notice, unknown to the world even by name, live only to lighten the burden of human misery?

In the late 1890s Charles Booth also noted the parochial work of the sisterhoods in London with approval.[36] Apart from Protestant suspicion of their churchmanship and the deep-rooted prejudice which fed on that suspicion, sisterhoods attracted one major criticism within the Victorian Church. They were widely considered too independent of the established pattern of ecclesiastical authority. Father Congreve observed in 1908 that 'the fact of a Sister's dedication to the virgin-life does not *per se* bring the dedicated persons into any peculiar relations

---

[36] Congreve, 'Sisters', p. 6; Great Britain, Parliamentary Papers, 1857–58, ix, *Report from the Select Committee of the House of Lords Appointed to Inquire into the Deficiency of Means of Spiritual Instruction and Places of Worship in the Metropolis and Other Populous Places in England and Wales: Especially in the Mining and Manufacturing Districts*, p. 172, 174; CCR (1873–78); Burgon, *Woman's Place*, pp. 11–12; Booth, *Religious Influences*, vii. 351.

with the Episcopate different from the relations they had before'. The sisterhood could elect its own Episcopal Visitor, thereby giving him authority over the community, but no bishop, no diocesan bishop, 'has an inherent right to be the Visitor'. Such a situation gave remarkable freedom to the sisterhood and power to its Superior; only when the sisters undertook 'diocesan or parochial works [were] they . . . bound to carry on . . . in loyal subordination to the diocesan or parochial authorities'. The independence of the situation caused some, in Convocation, to press (unsuccessfully) for a Church-wide rule for sisterhoods which could be enforced throughout the institution. The bishops hoped that 'recognised relations to Episcopate' could be worked out, and the diocesan bishop would generally be the Visitor providing an 'appeal from the autocratic rule of the Superior'. In 1895 the Sisters of the Church (Kilburn) were still without a Visitor and the bishops noted 'there was no proper episcopal or regular ecclesiastical control or supervision'. In fact this Community barely avoided censure by the bishops in 1895 for its extreme independence. The problem was tackled by a committee of the Lambeth Conference of 1897 which made rather modest recommendations to the constituent Anglican Catholic churches. The committee, significantly, observed that the need for communal independence resided precisely in the very quality of its central work: 'however important may be the work which is done for the Church by Brotherhoods and Sisterhoods, their primary motive is personal devotion to the Lord; and the development of the spiritual life is the power upon which the best active work depends'. In the same year the Lambeth Conference itself passed a resolution (No. 11) recognizing 'with thankfulness the revival alike of Brotherhoods and Sisterhoods and of the office of Deaconess in our branch of the Church'.[37]

---

[37] Congreve, 'Sisters', pp. 7–8; CC, 9 July 1861; Bishops' Meeting, Book 3, 4 Feb. 1885 (Lambeth Palace Library, London); Bishops' Meeting, Book 3, 19 June 1895; *The Five Lambeth Conferences* (London, 1920), 215–16; *The Lambeth Conferences (1867–1948): The Reports of the 1920, 1930 and 1948 Conferences with Selected Resolutions from the Conferences of 1867, 1878, 1897 and 1908* (London, 1948), 288.

Officially, deaconesses were revived in the modern Church of England when Elizabeth Ferard was commissioned (i.e. ordained) by A. C. Tait, bishop of London, in 1861, and much was made of the biblical precedents for this move. It was seen as a re-establishment of an ancient order, a revival under contemporary conditions and discipline of the function apparently once held by Phoebe in the Apostolic Church and confirmed later on in the Church both East and West, although subsequently dropped in medieval times. Although this historical rationale was important to early publicists of the Anglican female diaconate, it is quite possible that the *Church Times* was correct (13 February 1925) when it remarked that 'we are apt to create spurious antiques. We copied the Lutheran Deaconess from Kaiserswerth and then spent vast erudition in identifying her with the Deaconess of the Primitive Church.'[38]

The Kaiserswerth model was established by Pastor Fliedner of that town in Germany in 1836 when he brought together a group of women devoted to church work. In a real sense those Lutheran 'deaconesses', living in community but without belief in the indelibility of the vows of their Order or total vocational commitment, were 'Sisterhoods minus the vows' or 'Protestant "Sisters of Charity"'. The dedication of such women was said not to be marked by an act or ritual 'to confer any [special] *character* . . . The deaconesses are simply . . . a voluntary society [*sic*] for common life and work which they may leave at the call of more urgent duties'. The author of *Women and their Work* in 1855 saw in this example 'some very good hints' for 'numbers of our single women' who wished to offer themselves for service but who could not manage the total immersion and life-long obligations of the conventual life.[39]

It was upon this model that an Anglican clergyman, William Pennefather, founded the so-called Mildmay

---

[38] Rom. 16: 1. See also C. N. Norton, 'Women Deacons', *Church Militant* (July 1927).

[39] *The Ministry of Women*, pp. 134, 135; *Women and Their Work* (London, 1855), 13.

deaconesses in London in 1860, a private community with no official connection to the Church of England. Fifteen years after its foundation the Mildmay Mission had fifty-six 'deaconesses', as well as sixteen probationers and thirty 'professional nurses', and operated twelve mission stations in the poorest parts of east London. By 1899 the Mildmay Mission had expanded to 250 workers including 'deaconesses' and 'nurses'. By this time, it accommodated itself more fully to the official arrangements and discipline of the Church of England. No longer did workers venture out to 'missions' on their own; now 'it is at the request of the clergy that our deaconesses undertake work in the different parishes . . . The primary work of those who go forth daily from the Deaconess House is systematic house to house visitation.' A report of life in the Mildmay training home ('The Willows'), which had about fifty students in 1899, describes a two-year course of preparation including 'bible study, needlework and sewing, the keeping of accounts and a certain amount of house-work, cooking and simple nursing' as well as a good deal of on-the-job practical training in district visiting, mothers' meetings, etc. In addition to its 'primary work', the Mission trained foreign missionaries and undertook considerable work among prostitutes (including operating a home for rescued women), a registry for the unemployed, and an orphanage.[40]

In 1917 the Mildmay Deaconess Home closed and became, as St Catherine's House, a training institution more closely than ever connected to the Church. In 1920 it seems that the old 'Mildmay deaconess' had disappeared as a distinct type, as had the remnants of their independent foundation. In that year a committee of the Lower House of Convocation (Canterbury) defined three types of deaconess, one of which owed its origin to this tradition. It was a tradition which sustained and supported women 'who desired to be as free as possible in their aims and methods and laid themselves out especially for social and educational work and were definitely opposed to the idea of celibacy, whether formally imposed or informally

[40] CCR (1875); *Mildmay Work from Year to Year* (London, 1899), 8–22.

accepted by those who became deaconesses'. By that time, deaconesses of this tradition had 'definitely become a Church of England Movement'.[41]

Deaconesses in the Lutheran–Mildmay tradition posed no threat to the doctrine of female subordination; deaconesses were simply parish workers with no pretensions, albeit with a confusing title. The problem, as well as the opportunity, came with the notion of a 'revival' of the Apostolic and early Church tradition of a female diaconate, sometimes known in the Victorian period as the 'Primitive Order of Deaconesses'; the deaconess was properly commissioned, even 'ordained' by the diocesan bishops under whom such deaconesses must serve. This was the 'official' deaconess of whom Elizabeth Ferard was the first. Shortly after commissioning, she became the head of the deaconess home in the metropolis called the North London Deaconess Institute which, in 1864, reported a membership of seven deaconesses and several probationers. In this early period the infant movement's greatest champion was Dean Howson of Wells; it was vigorously backed by the two greatest Evangelical London parish priests of the period, William Cadman and W. W. Champneys, and was supported by a committee of ladies of substance, who helped raise money for the cause. By the mid-seventies there were deaconess training homes in six dioceses and commissioned deaconesses were accepted by several bishops. Yet the numbers of official deaconesses grew very slowly. Twenty years after the first 'ordination', official church deaconesses numbered only 60; and by 1920, in the English Provinces of Canterbury and York, there were only some 300, declining to 216 by 1930.[42]

The official deaconesses, from Elizabeth Ferard on, were 'set apart' (although the mode was unofficial and it varied from diocese to diocese), and there was a strong strain in the movement which saw this commissioning as life-long and as necessarily withdrawing the individual from

---

[41] *Guardian*, 2 Aug. 1917; Lambeth Conference Proceedings, 13 July 1920, LC 1920, cxxx, Minutes of Committee E (Lambeth Palace Archives).

[42] *Guardian*, 30 Nov. 1864; Edwin A. Pratt, *A Woman's Work for Women* (London, 1898), 8–11; CCR (1875), (1885); Lambeth Conference Proceedings, 28 July 1930, LC 147, remarks of Cyril F. Garbett.

ordinary life including marriage and family experience. Thus Deaconess Gilmore wrote a paper for the Pan-Anglican Congress of 1908 in which she stated, 'those . . . who are admitted . . . cannot be dispensed from it as from a vow, but they receive character which is life-long . . . they must be widows or virgins and . . . should be socially gentlewomen of education, of some means'. In a way very different from that of the Mildmay tradition, such women obviously saw themselves as in Holy Orders, and many of them lived in community dressed rather as if they were sisters. In other cases, the deaconesses, although equally dedicated, worked and lived as individuals under diocesan and parish leadership. The matter of possible marriage remained open although it seems that celibacy was generally favoured by those who took a high view of the office. In 1920, a Lambeth Committee, however, made it plain that 'no promise of celibacy is required for admission to the Order of Deaconess'.[43]

The official deaconess was tied very closely to the church structure, and in a cleary subordinate capacity. Remarking on the differences between sisters and deaconesses in 1868 Berdmore Compton remarked that whereas 'a sisterhood . . . is a private institution . . . in no respect bound to conform to any general system of regulation . . . the Deaconess Institution professes to be, and desires to be, part of the framework of the Church'. Over and over again this characterization of a deaconess as a woman 'under authority' is praised as a virtue. Thus in 1875 the Revd Arthur Gore spoke of the deaconess's connection to the pastor of a parish as 'in the relation which the trained nurse stands to the doctor. He is the head, she the ministering hand . . . Through her he has the confidence of his people, the knowledge of their difficulties and wants.' To an objective observer, Charles Booth, it was clear that 'the work undertaken by the deaconesses . . . is subordinated to that of the parish'. He spoke of the 'note of helpful subordination' which was continually sounded,

[43] Isabella Gilmore, 'Deaconesses: Their Qualifications and Status', in *Pan-Anglican Papers* (London, 1908), 2; see also *Papers Given at a Conference Convened by The Central Committee of Women's Church Work and The Head Deaconesses Association* (London, 1972).

and he listed some six deaconess centres or homes from which such work radiated in late Victorian London. [44]

Curiously, ecclesiastical authority showed great reluctance to give this obedient and subservient 'Order' a regular place in the church structure. There was general approbation of the deaconess ideal in Church Congresses and elsewhere. In 1871 a group of bishops drew up some 'Principles and Rules' to regulate the 'Order'; twenty years later the Convocation of Canterbury argued that 'it is desirable to encourage the foundation of Deaconess Institutions and the work of Deaconesses in our dioceses and parishes'. The bishops' meeting in 1894 agreed that individual deaconesses should be licensed to individual parishes and asked that this wish be transmitted to all diocesan clergy. Nothing apparently was done to implement this suggestion and, despite acknowledgement of the 'Order' by the Lambeth Conference of 1897, its uncertain status continued and remained through the First World War. In an appendix to the Archbishop's report on the *Ministry of Women* in 1919, Dr H. D. W. Stanton remarked that 'there is yet no official recognition of the status and duties of a deaconess in the English Church, nor any one authorised form of ordination', and somewhat loosely described the deaconess as 'a woman set apart by a bishop under that title for a service in the Church'. It was, in fact, through the effort to define her distinctive ministry within the Church and to determine the nature of her ordination that the deaconess became a vehicle for advancing the women's movement during the post-war years. [45] Within the parishes to which they were assigned by their bishops deaconesses worked as lay women, in visitation ('soon the deaconess will become a sort of mother to the parish' wrote Deaconess Gilmore in 1909), in Sunday school and girls' baptism and confirmation classes, in the care of the sanctuary (providing altar

[44] B. Compton, *Deaconesses* (London, 1868), 17; CCR (1875), 59; Booth, *Religious Influences*, vii. 350. See also CCR (1875).

[45] *The Ministry of Women*, p. 202; Bishops' Meeting, Book 3, 22 May 1894 (Lambeth Palace Library); Resolution 11, 1897, *The Lambeth Conferences (1867–1948)*, p. 288; Bishops' Meeting, Book 4, 1 June 1897; Bishops' Meeting, Book 4, 21 June 1905; *The Ministry of Women*, p. 190.

breads and linens), and in maintaining contact between the Church and all sorts of secular parish officials and societies.[46]

For this familiar supportive pastoral ministry (so like that of other late-Victorian full-time church workers) the deaconesses were trained in 'homes'. By the time of the Archbishop's Report on the *Ministry of Women*, there were ten functioning diocesan training homes for deaconesses, most of which apparently also trained ordinary lay parish workers and women foreign missionaries. No candidate for deaconess training was accepted until she reached the age of twenty-three, and she could not be ordained until she had reached thirty. Although little is said in the twentieth century about their social position, Sister Emily made it clear in 1894 that deaconesses ought to be of 'good education' and 'of some means'. The course of training occupied two years. In 1911 the Head Deaconess of Winchester Diocese (Mary Siddall) pointed out that this was a period of 'testing' as well as 'training'; should the candidate not 'feel called to a life-long service' she could still serve the Church but without being commissioned as a deaconess. Even after the two year training, actual ordination awaited a sort of 'curacy', a period of further testing in a parish situation. Training during the two intensive years was practical, intellectual, and devotional, the first taking about half of the available time during each day and involving practical parochial work such as visiting, Sunday school activities, mothers' meetings, and so on, as well as Charity Organisation Society theory and practice. The intellectual requirements were based on 'a sound knowledge of the Bible, Christian Dogma and Church History'. Deaconess Siddall was careful to point out that this was a general training only and that some deaconesses called to special ministries (e.g. trained nurses or teachers of theology) would need more academic preparation. Devotional discipline was essential, of a simple character which could be sustained by the deaconess in parochial isolation; the training home should be thought of as a diocesan centre of devotion which

[46] CCR (1909), 491–2.

would attract its graduates to some sort of communal life in their later years. In the third element of training, devotion, was included not only prayer but poise, i.e. 'readiness to meet any difficulty or emergency'.[47]

Although early twentieth-century deaconess training seems extensive for the period, not all informed contemporaries were impressed with its products. In his *Church Work* in 1905, Bernard Reynolds commented that 'the deaconesses need far more doctrinal and scriptural training than they have ever received in England'; in this connection he suggested that 'incalculable harm has been done to the Church by work that has been assumed without due study'.[48]

That the deaconess movement had problems was obvious by the time the Archbishop's Report on the *Ministry of Women* was written and published just after the War. The Revd H. D. W. Stanton listed several 'causes of slow development' in his paper published as an Appendix to that Report. One was 'lack of collective recognition by the Church', the result of uncertainty about the object of such recognition: 'there is no accepted definition of the office and no common formula of ordination'. Another, closely associated with the first, was the confusion which attached to the office, described as it was by some as a genuine participation in the Catholic Order of Christian Ministry, and by others simply as acceptance of a particular vocation as a special kind of lay worker.[49] Recognition and definition, these related problems, were to draw the deaconess movement, so modest in extent and so deferential by tradition, into the centre of Church feminist controversy during the 1920s.

---

[47] *The Ministry of Women*, pp. 187–8; CCR (1909), 492; CCR (1894), 252; Paper Read by Head Deaconess Siddall to a *Conference on November 2, 1911 Convened by The Central Committee of Women's Church Work and the Head Deaconesses Association* (London, 1912), 7–11; *Deal* (June 1914), 224. See also CCR (1909).

[48] Bernard Reynolds, *Church Work* (London, 1905), 89–90.

[49] *The Ministry of Women*, p. 196.

PART II

The Movement towards Equality

4

Sources of Church Feminism

BEFORE Victorian times the Church of England had no professional ministry in the modern sense. There was, of course, an ordained ministry, and clergymen of the Church performed liturgical, homiletic, and pastoral functions as these were (and are) described in the Ordinal attached to the Book of Common Prayer. Until well into the nineteenth century, however, these functions were not thought to require specialized theological, pastoral, or practical training and practitioners were not required to achieve a measured standard of theological knowledge or pastoral skill. A clergyman took orders with his whole professional duty to learn; he undertook his ministerial work as an amateur. He also took on other amateur—and secular—roles. Clerical incumbents, for example, were quite likely to be appointed justices of the peace. The vicar often provided such medical aid as was available in a village and he usually controlled most of the charitable and educational resources of the community. His role was a diffuse one, and the religious side of it was not clearly differentiated from those parts which attached to his social position as a gentleman. In the late eighteenth century, gentleman and parson were very closely allied, the profession and the status were scarcely separable.

By the mid-Victorian years all this had changed. In very large part the English parson had become a professional man.[1] He was likely to have been educated (though perhaps modestly) in theology and trained (though perhaps without much system) pastorally. He met with his fellow clergymen throughout his career in clerical societies and conferences. He might be involved in the developing

---

[1] For discussions of the professionization of the clergy of this period see Anthony Russell, *The Clerical Profession* (London, 1980) and Brian Heeney, *A Different Kind of Gentleman* (Harnden, Conn., 1976).

self-government of the church, possibly in one of the Convocations, more likely in a diocesan conference or a rural deanery meeting. He had available a large and increasing professional literature, both books and periodicals, and he dressed distinctively, so that his outward appearance was no longer that of other men. The most significant change of all was that he had come to concentrate his energies on his clerical duties in their narrower definition, that is on what the sociologist Anthony Russell calls the 'charter role' of the clergyman as set out in the Ordinal.[2] As he concentrated on his specialized professional role, many of the clergyman's traditional tasks dropped away. Gone were the days when he functioned happily as a magistrate or as a politician, or when he doctored the sick and gave advice on any matter that came to his notice. Other professional men had stepped into these roles; accredited country doctors and solicitors, registrars, party agents, policemen, trained teachers, and a host of government officials.[3]

The clergyman's 'charter role', on Russell's definition, had three main aspects: leadership in public worship, preaching, and pastoral care. The first included the daily offices, Sunday duty, sacramental services, and the rites of passage. The second consisted primarily of the preparation and delivery of sermons at regular and special services. The third was made up principally of regular house-to-house visiting, the visitation of the sick and bereaved, private counselling, instruction and teaching in parochial schools and institutions; in fact it included all professional contact with parishioners outside the appointed services of the Church.

Victorian laywomen were only passively associated with the first two aspects of ordained professional ministry in the Church of England. It seems that they made up the majority of worshippers (at least towards the end of the nineteenth century) and predominated among sermon-attenders. They neither led nor assisted in leading public worship in church buildings; nor did they occupy pulpits

[2] Russell, *Clerical Profession*, pp. 38, 63, 85, 103, 234–5.
[3] Ibid., 234.

or speak in churches. Victorian laymen, on the other hand, participated not only as members of choirs, but also as servers, assisting the priest at Holy Communion; from the 1860s onwards they could become layreaders, and, as such, eventually gained the right to preach at regular services.[4]

The only approach made by Victorian women towards the charter role of the clerical profession was, as we have seen, through its third or pastoral side. The whole process of visiting the poor in their homes gave district visitors, bible and mission women, deaconesses, and sisters attached to parishes a stake in the active pastoral ministry of the Victorian Church of England. Visiting gave them opportunities to interview individuals and families, to organize girls and women into appropriate clubs, to found savings banks and provident societies, and to establish lines of communication between parish priests and their parishioners.

It is hardly surprising that the first rustlings of a new women's consciousness, the first stirrings of real desire to be professional church workers, should show themselves in a series of moves to encourage the better preparation of laywomen pastoral auxiliaries, especially as teachers and parish visitors. In 1901, Louise Creighton, widow of the bishop of London, wrote that neither lady volunteers nor paid working-class biblewomen, nor even deaconesses, could do what a new-style church worker would do. The new worker, she wrote, would be an educated woman 'thoroughly trained and competent' with 'greater responsibility and independence in the organization of the work amongst the women and children in the parish'. It would be her task to encourage and expand the corps of voluntary workers, 'organizing the work of others, bringing in new workers, finding the proper place for each, smoothing out difficulties and guiding the inexperienced'. Above all, the new-style woman church worker was not to be simply a subordinate creature. She 'should not be merely a parochial drudge, but a fellow-worker with the

---

[4] Chadwick, *Victorian Church*, ii. 222–3; Booth, *Religious Influences*, vii. 424; Mudie-Smith, *The Religious Life of London*, pp. 267, 443.

clergy, within her own sphere, and subject of course to the control of the head of the parish'.[5]

In 1894 Mrs Creighton referred to the old view of women's place in the world, in which 'the ideal for women was a sheltered existence; the great battle of life in the world was to be fought by men. Women . . . were to be kept ignorant of sin and evil.' But now that a woman had much more 'independence, self respect, security of her own position, the less she will exert herself or attract unworthy men'. Part of the old mission of women, and part of the new as well, was, as we have seen, subordination, and in particular subordination to the parish priests.[6]

Where there were differences between the parish priest and the women working for him it was felt that the difficulty could 'best be met by resolution on the ladies' part not to transgress the pastor's orders'.[7] To many, this type of woman seemed out of date in the period at the beginning of the First World War, for 'side by side with the ideal of the woman who devotes herself exclusively to husband, home, and children', there had arisen the ideal of 'the woman who is economically independent'. In the year after the war began, the *Guardian* (21 October 1915) gave a number of reasons why the independent work of women was becoming more important. It remarked on the absence of bridegrooms for every woman available, on the effect of the income-tax on parents, on the need for soldiers and veterans' wives to work, and on 'the experience of the real joy of work which has come to many women during the war . . . they have experienced reality, they have lived, they will not go back to golf, to bridge, to seeing the shops and listening to the band'. The newspaper went on to prophesy: 'we might see in the future, women as the privates in the industrial army while men are the officers'. Yet the war was but one reason for the acceleration of the women's movement; it was not the only source of attitudinal change. Some months before

---

[5] Chadwick, *Victorian Church*, ii. 163–5; Creighton, 'The Work of Women in the Parish' in *Laity in Council*, pp. 121–3, 136.

[6] CCR (1894), Mrs Creighton, p. 240.

[7] Yonge, *Womankind*, p. 291.

the war broke out, on 7 January 1914, the *Christian Common-wealth* remarked that 'women are beginning to take religion very seriously and to demand the resolute appli-cation of the logic of Christianity to their present position . . . There is a significant contrast between this grave and challenging attitude and the traditional meekness and emotionalism which has hitherto been the mark of feminine religion.'[8] Thus even before the war broke out the idea of women's work had begun to change its form. The frame-work of thought which surrounded women's role contributed substantially to the position in which women found themselves. Among the most obvious requirements for women in the period before the First World War was training. This was evident in almost all the writing and speaking on the subject of volunteers.

Mrs Humphry Ward, in a panegyric on Mrs Creighton's biography of her husband wrote, 'what strikes one par-ticularly about this whole movement is that it is a move-ment in favour of training'. She spoke, of course, of the women's movement in general. At a 1909 Church Congress, Canon Denton Thompson remarked that 'definite instructions and systematic training' would be required not only in religious subjects specifically but also in social subjects. Workers should be able to 'interest girls in the anatomy of their bodies, the function of their organs, and kindred subjects'. In the same pre-war flurry about training, Mrs Creighton, Mrs Gertrude Tuckwell, and Mrs Chaloner Chute of the GFS made substantial con-tributions. Mrs Chaloner Chute, the GFS president, said the Society 'had been able to give much help and infor-mation to the women officials of labour bureaus, besides doing a great deal of work in making enquiries and finding suitable work situations for girls, especially on the Continent'. The bishop of Stepney (Henry Luke Paget) remarked in 1913 that the Women's Diocesan Association 'urged the need of serious preparation, and something like adequate remuneration'. He went on to recommend 'at least two years of definite training plus an examination'. In

[8] Zoë Fairfield, *The Woman's Movement and the Family* (London, 1913), p. 191; *Christian Commonwealth*, 7 Jan. 1914.

the next year the *Guardian* itself commented, 'Church workers . . . had to labour side by side with civic workers, with sanitary inspectors, nurses, health visitors, teachers in day schools—all especially trained for their special vocations—and for the Church Worker who had to deal with social, economic and religious questions, careful training was equally necessary.'[9]

The first effort to acquire training of an adequate and reasonable type for women was that of a single training institution. Effort was made during the war by the Central Committee of Women's Church Work in 1916 and 1917. The proposal was taken up urgently by men of a progressive cast such as William Temple who wrote,

we need . . . more of the Church Women than we already know; and we need that more scope should be given to them; as, for example, that they should, when suited, be entrusted with a large part of the training of candidates for Confirmation. We believe that if such an agency were made, more women, and more highly qualified women, would offer themselves for this form of service . . . The Church must learn to take all life as its province and make definite provision for all those who are to do good work of any sort. For this purpose there must be training; and we must desire to see a Church Training College with a high standard of efficiency, preparing women for Church work, for general social work, and perhaps for foreign mission work.[10]

In the course of time, the idea of a central training institute disappeared, both in the Church Women's Committee and the Church at large. In the place of a central college grew up the idea and the reality of an Inter-Diocesan Council on training in which men were heavily represented. During the 1920s there was a real effort to create a standard of training throughout the Church for women, an effort which was responded to by much community energy. In 1921 several old centres survived, of which St Catherine's—the

[9] Mrs Humphry Ward, paper in Pusey House Library, Oxford; CCR (1909), Canon Denton Thompson, p. 451; (1910), Mrs Chaloner Chute, 496; Bishop of Stepney in the *Guardian*, 30 May 1913; *Guardian*, 25 June 1914.

[10] Central Committee of Women's Church Work, 5 Dec. 1916, 7 June 1917 Minute Book, Church House Archives, London; William Temple, 'Co-operation in Social Work' in C. C. B. Bardsley (ed.), *Women and Church Work* (London, 1917), 50.

old Mildmay Centre for Deaconesses—was perhaps the most prominent. As these developed and other centres were opened, the question of a standard of 'recognition' naturally arose. It was agreed that it should be given to specialized workers in (a) teaching, (b) rescue work, and (c) social work, and general recognition be given to those showing proof of training in both theological and social work. At first the Council concerned itself only with the dioceses of London, Southwark, and Chelmsford. Later in the decade more dioceses were taken into the care of the Council. In 1921 the Inter-Diocesan Council for Women's Work was given the status of an entry in the *Official Year-book of the Church of England*. It was then noted that 'certificates of recognition are given to trained workers by the *Inter-Diocesan Council for Women's Work* which is the result of friendly co-operation between the Boards of Women's Work and the Dioceses [London, Winchester, Chelmsford, and Southwark]'. The co-operative venture in training represented by the Inter-Diocesan Council continued through the 1920s, and by 1930 some 700 women received the diploma in theology which reflected its agreed standards. Throughout the entire period from 1912, women were able to take the Archbishop's examination in theology, an examination which raised them to the standard of Oxford and Cambridge theology. The sub-committee for the Central Council for Women's Church Work, founded in 1930, inspected the results of the various training homes or colleges for women throughout the country. The principle of inspection was accepted, and the effort to establish a separate central training college for women consequently abandoned. In 1930 'Rules of Procedure for the Inspection of Training Centres Deserving Recognition' were established, and it was determined that there should be two inspectors, one man and one woman. In addition to the 'course of training' and 'the particular purposes for which a house exists' the sub-committee was to consider 'the constitution and function of the governing body' and 'the suitability of each House as a training centre'. Enquiry should be made as to accommodation and domestic arrangements, diet, leisure and recreation, general routine and discipline, and the scope for the development of initiative; opportunity for study was to be made, as well as provision for the devotional 'life and for spiritual help'.[11] The worth of this Committee will be further examined in Chapter 6.

Throughout the nineteenth century there had been tension between the domestic ideal and the development of women's independent work. Despite the growth of the latter, the ideal of domesticity and the supreme aim of motherhood usually took first place, following Sarah Austin who in 1857 noted, 'take it at whichever end of the social scale you will, there is nothing higher than this: the comfort, order and good government of the house and the instruction of the young'. On the other hand, throughout this period there was some question about the position of the family in relation to women's independence. For example, Florence Nightingale was Cassandra in 1859, and both J. H. Blunt and F. P. Cobbe questioned the domestic ideology in the 1860s. Moreover, writers frequently made the point that the responsibility of parenthood is a dual one, 'the man and the women together, each supplying what is lacking in the other, the man the head of the woman, the woman the heart of the man'. The conflict between the old views of domesticity as the woman's role and the new view of independence and individuality as a part of the woman's role conflicted.

On the one hand were defenders of the traditional position such as the Dean of Manchester and Canon Thompson. In 1890, the Dean advised: 'make a bright, clean and cheerful home for your husbands and do what you can to prove to them both by training your children and your own life, that they have a rich reward'.[12] At the

11 *Minute Book 187*, 'Training College, 1919–22'; *Church of England Year-book* (1921), 237 ff.; *Guardian*, 28 Aug. 1919; *Church of England Year-book* (1921), p. 237; *Church Times*, 28 Mar. 1930; *Guardian*, 20 Feb. 1914; Sub-committee on Training House, *Minute Book 167, First Meeting*, 1 Oct. 1930; Committee on Training, Minute Book 167.

12 Austin, *Two Letters on Girls' Schools and on the Training of Working Women*, p. 20; see also Yonge, *Womankind*; see CCR (1878), Dr Bedell, Bishop of Ohio, 340; Butler, *Woman's Work and Woman's Culture*; Blunt, *Directorium Pastorale* (London, 1864); F. P. Cobbe, 'The First Cause of Women' in Butler, *Woman's Work and Woman's Culture*; Yonge, *Womankind*, p. 31; Prochaska, *Women and*

Church Congress of 1909 the Canon admonished, 'the primary sphere of the ministry of women is unquestionably in the home'. On the other hand, in the same period, and also in the years after the First World War, the number of speakers who pressed for particular work for women was greater than ever before. Very prominent in many quarters in this particular instance was Louise Creighton. Speaking at the end of her address to the International Congress of Women in 1899, she remarked characteristically, 'the fitting her to earn her own living, did not of itself unfit her from becoming the very best wife and mother possible'. Speaking two years later to the Brighton Conference of the National Union of Women Workers she remarked that as a result of improved education women 'now for the most part are prepared to maintain that they have as much right as men to lead their own lives and to develop to the full their own capacities and to cease therefore to be mere appendages of men'. Her view had been shared by her husband: he agreed that professional life was compatible with good motherhood. He heartily remarked that the Mothers' Union and the Girls' Friendly Society 'aimed at uplifting the purity of the home' and that these organizations were growing very fast at the end of the nineteenth century. Between 1900 and 1930 several schools of thought were expressed. One was the very common one that it was possible to combine loyalty to the home and family with a new individuality for women. Thus, for example, Mrs Runciman said in 1912 that

there was no antagonism between ['citizenship and the home'] . . . the superior days of a woman were, and always would be, centred in her home. But there was no reason for women who were wives and mothers to forget that they were also citizens. Narrow and selfish homes did not breed public-spirited men and women. Every home had its share in the national life, and the more women could take part in the duties of citizenship the greater would be the sense of citizenship in the home.

Many believed that advancement in the enfranchisement of women would mean an advance in the quality of their

Philanthropy, p. 219; CCR (1890), Bishop of Manchester, Meeting of Working Women, p. 617.

home role. Others such as Sophia Langwood in the *Guardian* of 27 March 1919 expressed the view that an increase in the individual role of women would develop their family role as well:

it is open to argument whether she [the middle-class housewife] is not just as well employed looking after her home and all the invaluable things appertaining thereto as working just as hard in the interests of philanthropy or charity in the world outside us. It is when she tries, as many do, to combine the two that she fails either in one or both. But if she makes up her mind to bring all her education to bear on her task of home-making and takes it up as her life-work she will by good organization and management be able to carry on.

There is no doubt too, as Mrs Creighton put it, that co-operation between the two parents would make individual work for the wife necessary and also possible. [13]

Theodore Parker, an American clergyman who frequently visited London pulpits, at an early stage (1853) raised a central objection to the

inadequacy of domesticity: [the] domestic function of woman as housekeeper, wife and mother, does not exhaust her powers, woman's function like charity begins at home; then, like charity, goes everywhere. To make one half of the human race conserve all their energies in the functions of housekeeper, wife, and mother, is a monstrous waste of the most precious material God ever made.

He went on to describe four types of women who needed public work in addition to their private domestic duties: first, the unmarried, i.e. the 'permanently unmarried'; second, the domestic women who 'drudge, wholly taken up in the material details of their housekeeping, husband-keeping and child-keeping. Their housekeeping is a trade and no more; and after they have done that there is no

[13] CCR (1909), Canon Denton Thompson, p. 477; see also Pan-Anglican Congress, 1908; Mrs Creighton on 'The Modern Home', *International Congress of Women: Women in Professions I* (London, 1899) p. 11; Mrs Creighton, 'The Modern Home. A Paper given at the Brighton Conference of the National Union of Women Workers' (London, 1901), p. 3; Creighton, *International Congress of Women: Women in Professions I*; CCR (1909), p. 487; Mrs Runciman, Queen's Hall Meeting (1912); see also *Church Times*, 13 Dec. 1912; letter from Sophia Langwood, *Guardian*, 27 Mar. 1919; Mrs Creighton in *Christian Commonwealth*, 26 June 1912.

more that they can do'; third, women with 'no taste and no talent for domestic function'; fourth, 'women who will be married but are not married yet'.

From the 1890s, a familiar theme of individual citizenship is articulated. Mrs Creighton observed in 1897 that 'it was in the home that woman's duty must first be done. But they ought not only to consider how to bear the home burdens. They must remember also that they were citizens.' In 1899 Alice E. Busk wrote on 'Women's Work on Vestries and Councils' in J. E. Hand's *Good Citizenship*; she wrote in detail of women's roles in various local government bodies in the Local Government Act of 1894. Mrs Creighton was a delegate to the International Congress of Women in 1899 when a great many vocations for women in social life were discussed: prisons and reformatories; preventive work; rescue work; treatment of people in the destitute classes; women's clubs; social settlements; equal moral standards for men and women; amusements; temperance; provident schemes; emigration; protection of young travellers; protection of bird and animal life. Although the Revd R. W. Harris insisted that 'your real influence does not lie in public power . . . it lies in the power you exert over men, individually and personally,' he went on to say, 'I should like to see women on Boards of all sorts.'

In 1922 Maude Royden received no less than four invitations to stand for Parliament, although in fact she accepted none of them. By 1924 there were eight women MPs. None the less, in the period after the war and indeed during the war itself, the view that women's work was dominantly domestic and motherly was predominant; and this predominance lasted until well into the twentieth century. Thus it was quite acceptable in Anglo-Catholic circles to argue the question of whether women should wear hats in church, or even to discuss the effects of menstruation. In the *Church Militant* on 15 May 1926 there was some dispute as to whether women should communicate before men, or after, to indicate their subordination. There was little question that women's nature was different from men's nature and that women's work was thus different. Some writers were very clear that women not only had a distinct and separate sphere, but that they also had an equal sphere to that of men. Mrs Richardson, for example, in her *Women of the Church of England* wrote that women 'is a being of a nature and vocation not merely supplementary but additional to man . . . they are called to be as a body "Sisters of Charity" . . . They are in fact to be regarded and to regard themselves as having something of the angel in them, as being among men but not of them.' [14] In the post-war period there were a number of people who went so far as to specify that women had a nature superior to that of men and vocations that were superior to those of men. But against this, Canon Streeter remarked at a Church Congress in 1919 that he would have felt it

necessary to attempt an elaborate justification for the proposal that the Church should make use of women in its official ministry. I should have felt it necessary to produce arguments to prove that the gifts of organization, public speaking, of leadership, of the power of constructive thought, etc. etc., were possessed by a sufficiently large number of women to make the proposal a practical one . . . [now] the world has seen women doctors, women teachers, women organizers, women municipal councillors, women orators, women thinkers, in sufficient numbers to prove that "intelligence" in these things is not a peculiarly masculine quality. [15]

There is no doubt that a serious effort to come together by women in various Church organizations occurred in the late nineteenth century and early twentieth century. The National Union of Women Workers and later the National Council of Women provided the focus for this union. By 1905, the National Council of Women had 120 affiliated societies and forty branches; twenty years later it passed the following resolution and forwarded it to the Bishops'

[14] Theodore Parker, *The Public Function of Women* (London, 1853), pp. 5–9; CCR (1897), Mrs Creighton, p. 487; Miss Alice E. Busk, 'Womens' Work on Vestries and Councils' in J. E. Hand, *Good Citizenship* (London, 1899); *International Congress of Women* (1899); CCR (1902), Revd R. W. Harris, p. 449; Maude Royden, 'Letters', Royden Papers, Fawcett Library, Box 222; *Church Militant*, 15 May 1926; *Christian Commonwealth*, 12 Apr. 1916; Richardson, *Women of the Church of England*, p. 301; see also Royden, *The Church and Woman* (London, 1924).

[15] CCR (1919), Streeter, p. 290–1.

Meeting: 'that this meeting . . . urged authorities of the Church to do all in their power to secure that a vocation to the Ministry of Religion shall receive official recognition, whether its possessor is a man or a woman'.[16]

In reaction to the various sources of Church feminism there were two distinctly positive types of response among Church women: the reaction which led some to challenge authority, and the reaction which led others to try to persuade authority that the new force of women's activity in the Church was a strong and valid power. Maude Royden and Louise Creighton, respectively, are excellent examples of these two sorts of reaction.

Maude Royden, who was an Anglican from birth, attended Cheltenham Ladies' College and Lady Margaret Hall, Oxford, before going to the Victorian Women's Settlement in Liverpool. She was a parish worker in the Revd Hudson Shaw's parish in Rutland, before being associated with him in the London slums during the war; she had also been an extension lecturer in English Literature for Oxford University in the early 1900s, during which time she became a strong and active advocate of women's suffrage. During the middle part of the war there was a serious controversy in England concerning the Mission of Repentance and Hope as to whether or not women should have a role in teaching and evangelizing. In the midst of this controversy Maude Royden accepted the Assistant preachership at the City Temple in London under Dr F. N. Newton, a Congregationalist. As 'E. M. J.' wrote in 1921, 'the generous spirit of the City Temple in offering Miss Royden a pulpit was paralleled by her supreme moral courage, a Church Woman [*i.e. an Anglican*] in accepting it. Her preaching filled the City Temple to the roof.' But not only did she preach; remarkably, she also baptized several children.

Shortly after the war, with Percy Dearmer, she founded the Guildhouse, an interdenominational gathering held once a week, eventually in a building in Eccleston Square. In addition to her work of preaching, which was very

[16] H. Pearl Adam (ed.), *Women in Council* and *The Jubilee Book of the National Council of Women of Great Britain* (London, 1945), pp. 18, 34–5.

substantial both in her own church and in Anglican ones, she was well known as a counsellor and as an advocate of speaking out on sex and other delicate subjects. She received a degree from the University of Edinburgh and during the period after 1930 she undertook several trips to America. Maude Royden's ambition was principally to fulfil her vocation despite the conditions in the Church of England. Nothing exhibits her attitude more perfectly than her confused relationship with the Bishop of London over her preaching at the Three Hour Good Friday Service in the period during the First World War and after. Although in fact the threat seemed to come to nothing there did appear in the press in 1917 some doubt as to Maude Royden's effectiveness in the City Temple.

I fear you have taken a disastrous step by consenting to preach at the City Temple. It will cause endless difficulties for all of us who are trying to do what we can to improve the position of women . . . If it is because you think the best way of having the law amended is to break it, are not these the methods of the W.S.P.U. only slightly modified as far as physical force is concerned? It seems to me that there is a sort of ecclesiastical militancy . . . I fear that Mr. Riley will rejoice exceedingly!

A clipping from the *Daily Chronicle* of 19 April 1919 describes the scene at St Botolph's Bishopsgate in 1919.

at the last moment the Bishop of London prohibited the Three Hour Service at St. Botolph's Bishopsgate being conducted by Miss Royden yesterday. When the congregation arrived at the Church they found a notice, signed by the Rev. W. Hudson Shaw on a board in front of the door [accepting the prohibition] . . . An invitation was extended by the Rector to those who came to the Church to attend the service in the adjoining parish room, where a service was to be taken by Miss Royden. A very large congregation was the result, the parish room being crowded, all the windows of the room were opened and crowds of worshippers gathered around each window.

In the same year Miss Picton-Turbervill became 'the first woman to preach in the Church of England at a statutory service.' Following Miss Royden's preaching in the parish room in 1919 a petition against her activities with 'over a thousand representative signatures' was circulated within ten days to the Bishop of London. On 19 April 1919 shortly after noon, worshippers coming into the Church of St Botolph's Bishopsgate, found a notice informing them that the Bishop had 'prohibited' the service and urging that 'this order of course will be obeyed'. Despite this setback, by 1921 Maude Royden's place as a preacher at St Botolph's was established. The *Daily Chronicle* reported on 26 March 1921,

ignoring the objection of the Bishop of London, Miss Maude Royden yesterday preached at the Three Hour Service at St. Botolph's. There was a very large congregation.
Before the service began, the Rector, The Rev. W. H. Shaw asked that anyone who had come to the Church to make a protest should rise at once, and having protested, should go away.

Maude Royden's preaching was thus in direct and calculated contradiction to the views and direction of the Bishop of London, and was consequently an important moment in the history of the assertion of women's rights in church. As the *Observer* put it, she decided to do it despite

the Bishop of London's statement that it is not only without his sanction, but against his expressed wish. It is not a statutory service . . . and Miss Royden considers . . . that there is nothing illegal in her taking it. Indeed both she and the Rector of St. Botolph's Bishopsgate consider that they are really fulfilling the conditions that were suggested in the Report of the Lambeth Conference, the recommendation being that women should be allowed to preach at non-sanctuary services . . . The statutory service for Good Friday will be held as usual at St. Botolph's and will in no way be interfered with by the Three Hour Service, but will follow and will be taken by Miss Royden at the Mid-day.

Despite the work of Maude Royden in St Botolph's Bishopsgate and W. Hudson Shaw's support of women preachers, a hostile amendment was passed, by 195 votes to 111, at the London Diocesan Conference in May 1921, which stated that it 'is generally inexpedient and contrary to the interests of the Church that women should publicly minister in consecrated buildings'. Miss Royden was willing to preach when she was able despite the directions of the House of Bishops, whereas most other women were only willing to do so with the permission of ecclesiatical authority. Some women, however, took the view of Maude Royden: for example, Miss Picton-Turbervill, who preached at Lincoln, Dublin, and Geneva (where she had local Episcopal sanction but not general Episcopal approval). It was reported of her that 'she adopts, when preaching, the cassock and surplice, taking the view that this is the most suitable clothing for one who is primarily a ministrant, a messenger, a voice'. Another woman preacher was Mrs St Clair Stobart, who, although refused permission to preach in churches by the bishop of London, did so in the City Temple and in various churches in the USA.[17]

Louise Creighton (1850–1936) was another characteristic member of the women's movement, but represented a rather different approach. The tenth child of a German Baltic merchant who settled in London, she became the wife of Mandell Creighton, who moved from a fellowship at Merton to a Northumberland parish, and then on to the chair of church history at Cambridge, before becoming bishop of Peterborough and then of London, where he died in 1901. Louise herself wrote a good deal of historical romance in Oxford, and a two-volume life of her husband in 1904. She was for a number of years vice-chairman of the Central Conference of Women's Church Work in London and from 1920 to 1930 was a member of the Church Assembly during its first ten years. She was the only woman member of the Joint Committee of the Insurance Commissioners appointed in 1912 and she was three times President of the National Council of Women Workers. Unlike Maude Royden, she worked within the Church establishment, and whenever possible used the machinery already given. She was tireless in addressing Church Congresses and gatherings of women at the Pan-Anglican Congress and at missionary gatherings. She was the

[17] *Dictionary of National Biography*, Maude Royden (1876–1956); obituary notices in *The Times*, 31 July and 2 Aug. 1956; A. M. Royden, *A Threefold Cord* (London, 1956); Francis C. Eeles to Maude Royden, 10 Mar. 1917, 'Letters', Royden Papers, Fawcett Library, Box 222, *Daily Mirror*, 1 July 1919; *Christian Commonwealth*, 14 May 1919; *Daily Express*, 19 Apr. 1919; *Observer*, 20 Mar. 1921; Report of Lambeth Conference (1919); *Church Times*, 27 May 1921; *Sussex Daily News*, 2 Feb. 1921; *Sunday Express*, 30 Jan. 1921; *The Times*, 3 July 1934.

leading woman in the Church of England during the first two decades of the twentieth century. A family woman with four daughters and three sons, she started the Mothers' Union in Peterborough after her husband's appointment there in 1891, and displayed a keen interest in the Girls' Friendly Society, in rescue work, and in causes 'directed to the welfare of women'. She was a member of the SPG Standing Committee and took the leading part in the Missionary Conference and in the Pan-Anglican Congress of 1908. Above all perhaps, Mrs Creighton was notable, particularly in her speeches, for her sense of the need for independence and individuality among women, but also of the value of maintaining a good family life. She is happily described by Virginia Woolf, 'I was pitched strangely enough into the arms of Widow Creighton who remembered me, she said . . . I found her easy enough; a sincere fine old thing, her face emerging out of a mist of flesh, and looking infinitely seared & worn like an immensely old sun shining through the mist.' Louise Creighton thus represented all that was best in moderate Anglican feminism; she was bold, practical and respectable. But her very virtues demonstrated the limitations of her position and of the Church she served.[18]

[18] *The Diary of Virginia Woolf, 1915–1918,* i (London, 1977), entry for 1 July 1918, p. 162.

5

Voice and Vote: Women in the Government of the Church

IN the lay woman's role in the Church of England in the early twentieth century, nothing occupied her attention more than playing a part in the Representative Church Council, the Parochial Church Council, or the intermediate conferences or diocesan synods which occupied their place. Late Victorian feminism was stimulated by the expansion of the male franchise in successive Reform Acts and by the growing participation of adult males in national politics. There is no evidence that this trend in the direction of a democratic system of representation had any more influence in hastening ecclesiastical change than did the widening of women's place in public life or the development of feminist theory; nevertheless, Church democracy matured more rapidly than did Church feminism. Whereas women's exclusion from the government and ministry of the Church continued and was little challenged before 1900, by the beginning of the new century lay men increasingly participated in ecclesiastical discussion and decision-making. The Church did not develop representative institutions before 1900, and the constitutional Church Assembly appeared only after World War I; yet the way was prepared in the previous fifty years as lay men took a growing part in discussions at Church Congresses, diocesan conferences, voluntary parochial councils, and the houses of laymen attached to the two Convocations.

In mid-Victorian times the Church felt threatened by militant dissenters committed to the disestablishment cause, a threat which Gladstone himself seemed to emphasize in

Parts of this chapter are taken from Brian Heeney, 'The Beginnings of Church Feminism: Women and the Councils of the Church of England, 1897–1919', *Journal of Ecclesiastical History*, 33 (January 1982), 89–109; those parts are reproduced with the kind permission of the journal's editorial board.

1885 in his address to the electors of Midlothian. Safe-
guarding the Establishment meant rallying the Church's
defenders, encouraging faithful laymen to co-operate with
bishops and clergy to ward off the evil day. From the early
1860s, annual Church Congresses provided regular national
occasions for such co-operation, for discussion of Church
defence and reform. The Congresses were not representative or authoritative bodies; votes were not taken at any of
their sessions, nor were decisions made. Anyone interested
in Church affairs could attend a Church Congress; women
were admitted at an early stage, although their contributions to discussion were expressed through male proxies
until 1885. In that year Miss Agnes Weston read her own
paper, a practice which was customary from then on.[1]

At the local level, the abolition of compulsory Church
rates in 1868, and the establishment of secular parish councils twenty-eight years later, stripped the vestries of their
general political interest and civil power. From the 1860s
bishops encouraged the formation of voluntary parish
councils for ecclesiastical purposes. As interest in these
gained momentum in the 1890s they became an important
means by which laymen were included in Church affairs at
the parochial level. Beginning at Ely in 1866, diocesan conferences extended this form of lay participation; by the early
1880s nearly all dioceses held such conferences regularly.[2]
In some places laymen shared in discussions at rural
deanery meetings as well. Under the leadership of Archbishop Benson, a lay house of the Canterbury Convocation
was created in 1885. Although it had no power and met
only to be consulted by the bishops and clergy, its regular
gathering from 1886 (1892 in York) marked yet another
advance in lay co-operation.

The early involvement of laymen in Church councils
was a response to external threat, an aspect of Church
defence against dissenters and disestablishment. From the
1890s the advocates of Church self-government, and of lay
co-operation, often took a more positive line. In 1896 the

[1] K. A. Thompson, *Bureaucracy and Church Reform* (Oxford, 1965), p. 92; CCR
(1885) pp. 80 ff. (speech by Miss Weston) and p. 164 (speech by Harvey
Goodwin).
[2] Chadwick, *The Victorian Church*, ii. p. 359–60.

Church Reform League was founded; a year later it
published a pamphlet entitled *Reform of the Church* in which
the cause of self-government within the framework of
Establishment was linked to sweeping reform of Church
patronage, discipline, and finance. The reform movement
was joined to social responsibility and even radicalism,
especially in the minds of liberal Anglo-Catholics Charles
Gore and Henry Scott Holland and, later on, in the person
of William Temple, the leading spirit in the Life and Liberty
movement of 1917. Just as the feminist cause blossomed in
Edwardian England and during the Great War, so the
movement for self-government in the Church, and for the
participation of laymen and women in that government,
matured in the twenty years before the Treaty of Versailles.[3]

On 13 May 1897 the bishops in the Upper House of
Canterbury Convocation adopted six resolutions designed
'to quicken the life and strengthen the work of the Church'
by encouraging the formation of parochial church councils.
The fourth proposal stipulated that 'elected councillors be
male communicants of the Church of England of full age'.
The bishops hesitated before accepting the word 'male'; a
move to delete it was defeated in fact by only two votes
Their evident reluctance to rule out the election of women
was caused by the bishop of Salisbury's revelation that he
had two female churchwardens in his diocese and by the
bishop of Chichester's assertion that there was 'an appreci-
able number' of women wardens.[4] As all churchwardens
were to be put on the proposed councils as ex-officio members, some bishops could see no reason to exclude women
who might achieve the same position by election.

It was this very close vote by the bishops that provoked
the first clear expression of Church feminism. In February
1898 a petition, signed by 1,100 churchwomen, was presented to the Upper House protesting against its ban on
female candidates for election to parochial church councils.
When the offending resolution of the previous May came
before the clergy in the lower House of Convocation on 4
February, this protest was very much in the minds of the

[3] Thompson, *Church Reform*, p. 138.
[4] CC (1897), 227, 213. The bishop of Salisbury was John Wordsworth
(1843–1911); the bishop of Chichester was E. R. Wilberforce (1840–1907).

debaters. Another effort was made to expunge the word 'male'. The anomaly of women's eligibility for ex-officio membership on councils as churchwardens was pressed hard. Furthermore, it was argued that country parishes would experience a shortage of suitable candidates for office were women to be excluded. Other more positive reasons were also brought forward for opening the councils to women. The Dean of St Paul's (Robert Gregory) pointed out that the new bodies were to deal with 'practical questions connected with parish matters', the very issues and affairs which women knew most about and on which they often made the largest contributions. Dean Gregory believed too that women were often 'the most devotional persons of the parish . . . the kind of people over whom the clergyman had most influence' and who could be most helpful to him. Members of Convocation need not fear that opening the councils to women committed them in the slightest degree on the issues or methods of the women's movement in secular politics. Gregory 'did not think that the female suffrage was the least involved' and he observed that women candidates for parochial councils 'would not be required to stand up and make speeches before they were elected, for it was hoped that the elections would be carried out on a far quieter system and would not require exhibitions of that sort'.

The Dean's arguments and assurances had very little effect on the ideas and fears of most of his colleagues in Convocation. Anxiety was more prominent than thought among the opponents of women councillors. Archdeacon R. P. Lightfoot feared that 'the most truly feminine women' would refuse to seek election. On the other hand if Convocation 'opened the door at all, there was no limit to the number of places on the council that women might occupy'. Would not a council 'composed very largely of women' be a weak instrument in local public affairs? Deeper questions bothered Archdeacon E. G. Sandford of Exeter. In his view women were not made by God to engage in public discussion, to debate and decide matters in a public forum, even a voluntary parochial church council without statutory powers. This sort of activity lay outside their proper sphere as it had been established by the Almighty and defined in Holy Scripture with admirable clarity by St Paul. Keen as he was to encourage women to work for the Church, he was determined to keep them out of those councils which, he thought, 'came near' to doing 'the governing work of the Church'. He saw a 'real danger lest the distinction between sex and sex should be forgotten', a danger very clear in view 'of the position of women now finding favour in many quarters'. He went on, 'The very fact that a large body of women were agitating in this very matter seemed to show that there was something behind and beyond the mere wish that had been expressed that day.'

Sandford and his allies easily won the debate and the exclusion of women from parochial church councils was maintained in the Lower House of Convocation by a vote of 39 to 18. The right of women to vote was never questioned. Sandford himself stated that 'no one would wish to exclude women from being amongst the electors of their Councils'. All voters, according to an agreed resolution, were to be *'bona fide* members of the Church of England, resident in the parish, and of full age'.[5]

By this deliberate decision of an all-male, all-clerical assembly, women were formally excluded from election to voluntary parochial church councils. The ban stood for sixteen years, although it was apparently sometimes overlooked.[6]

The exclusion was much resented by Louise Creighton. At the Church Congress in 1899, she chaired a session on 'The Training and Payment of Women Church Workers'. She asked why it was that 'in these days the best women do not devote their energies to what may, strictly speaking, be called Church work'? Among the answers she offered to this question was the failure of Church leaders to sympathize with the women's movement. Although Church leaders 'welcomed the establishment of sisterhoods and

[5] CC (1898), 123–7; CC (1897), 227 (Resolution 5).

[6] For evidence that women did sometimes sit on PCCs, see the *Guardian* 29 Nov. 1905 (speech by Bishop Gore in Representative Church Council). Report of Proceedings (hereafter cited at RCC); *Guardian*, 24 Nov. 1911 (speech by Earl Nelson in RCC).

encouraged means by which women might help the work of the clergy in their parish, they looked jealously on any-thing like independence of work or opinion on the part of women'. This attitude, she stated, was evident 'in the movement which would exclude women from the membership of Church Councils, a movement which . . . must tend to alienate thinking women from parish work', and had the disastrous effect of sharply separating the 'more advanced modern women' from the Church.[7]

Church feminism was created by this skirmish over rep-resentation on parochial church councils. It was established by the protracted and confusing debate about women's right to vote indirectly for members of the Representative Church Council, the unofficial precursor of the Church Assembly.

Enthusiasts for Church self-government were encouraged when, in 1899, Arthur Balfour declared in Parliament his desire to see 'greater spiritual autonomy' given to the Church of England. However, an attempt by Sir Richard Jebb to persuade the House of Commons to pass a 'Con-vocation Bill' providing for an authoritative Church legis-lature with lay representation failed in 1900, and it was clear that the direct parliamentary route to Church reform was blocked. Unwilling to facilitate self-government, Parliament could not itself find time to deal with Church matters.[8] It was this parliamentary incapacity, rather than theoretical belief in spiritual autonomy, which persuaded Archbishop Randall Davidson that the Church must be enabled to govern itself, though within the framework of the Establishment. In 1902 the two Convocations and their associated Houses of Laymen decided to meet together the following July in order to create a representative legislative body. It would have no statutory power and could pass no

[7] CCR (1849), 127–8.
[8] P. V. Smith, *Church Self-Government* (London, 1920), 8. Balfour was Leader of the House of Commons in 1899. Jebb (1841–1905) was a Conservative 'strongly opposed to legislative interference with the Established Church'; Michael Stenton and Stephen Lees, *Who's Who of British Members of Parliament*, ii (Hassocks, 1978), 191. P. V. Smith (1845–1929), a distinguished ecclesiastical lawyer and ardent churchman, calculated that 'out of 217 Church bills introduced into the House of Commons between 1888 and 1913, 33 were passed, 183 were dropped, and one was negatived'. *Church Self-Government*, p. 8.

laws for the Church, but churchmen believed it might commend itself to Parliament and achieve constitutional status in the future.

The joint meeting of six 'houses'[9] met in July 1903 and considered, among other things, the question of how, and by whom, the lay delegates to the Representative Church Council were to be elected, i.e. the 'lay franchise'. As a part of this discussion the women's franchise in Church elections was raised.

The issue of women serving as representatives on the proposed Council was never argued in 1903. It was agreed that 'representatives elected by the lay electors shall be of the male sex', hardly surprising in view of the ineligibility of women for the office of councillor even at the parish level.[10] On the other hand, women had been accustomed to vote for representatives in those parishes which had adopted voluntary councils, and it was not unreasonable for them to expect the vote in the election of lay representatives to higher councils, whether diocesan or national.

This was not to be. A scheme, drafted to include some female voters, was brought to the joint meeting of Convocation and Lay Houses in July 1903. It contained a proposal for a dual 'initial franchise': men were eligible either as 'qualified to vote at the election of churchwardens' or simply as communicants; women, on the other hand, were denied the second option. Thus, fulfilment of a spiritual requirement only (communicant status) would give the vote to men. Women, no matter how committed to the Church, no matter how hard-working in parochial affairs, could achieve the parish franchise only as occupiers or ratepayers, on an entirely secular basis.[11]

Lord Hugh Cecil, perhaps the most eloquent opponent of the women's cause, launched an attack on this double standard. The proposers of the draft franchise, he argued, 'were making the household qualification the true Church qualification, because by drawing a distinction between

[9] The Upper and Lower Houses of both Convocations, together with the two Houses of Laymen.
[10] CC (1904), Committee Report Number 385, p. 5.
[11] CC (1903), Committee Report Number 377, p. 3.

women householders and women communicants they made out that to be a householder was more important from a Church point of view than to be a communicant'. To eliminate this inconsistency, Lord Hugh moved that the franchise be confined to male communicants only. By a vote of 90 to 60 the joint meeting of the two Convocations and Houses of Laymen accepted this amendment and so decided to exclude women entirely from any share in the selection of lay delegates to the first Representative Church Council. The success of Lord Hugh's amendment did more than this. Election of lay delegates to the Representative Church Council was to be indirect; they were to be chosen at diocesan conferences by laymen, who in turn were elected by parochial church councils. Consequently the 'initial franchise' from which women were excluded in 1903 was that for members of parochial church councils, a suffrage they had hitherto exercised in parishes which had established such councils.[12]

Reaction among churchwomen and those churchmen who had espoused their cause was strong. At the Church Congress in October 1903 Charles Gore (then bishop of Worcester) described the exclusion of women from the Church suffrage as 'a great act of injustice'. Were it allowed to stand, 'schoolmistresses, district visitors, the parson's wife, the squire's wife, and many others who have been the very mainstay of the life of the Church . . . [would] be excluded from expressing their opinions in the election of the representatives. At the same Congress Mrs Arthur Philp, honorary secretary of the Mothers' Union in Worcester and secretary of the Ministering Children's League, representing, she said, 'women in the North and the Midlands', expressed the deep hurt and offence felt by even the most conservative churchwomen. She had no

[12] Report of Joint Meeting of the Members of the Convocation of Canterbury and York (sitting in Committee) and of the Houses of Laymen, held on 9 and 10 July 1903, p. 51. Lord Hugh Cecil, Baron Quickswood (1869–1956), was a prominent and controversial Conservative MP and author of *Conservatism* (London, 1912). A prominent member of the Representative Church Council, he continued as a leading member of the Church Assembly between the wars. He took a far more detached (and to a degree even a supportive) view of women's parliamentary suffrage than he did of the parallel Church issue; see Brian Harrison, *Separate Spheres: The Opposition to Women's Suffrage in Britain* (London, 1978), 242.

desire 'to be upon any Church Council, or to speak in any public places'; but to be denied the vote was an insult to women whose 'Churchmanship was their whole life'. She urged the men responsible to 'take . . . every means you can to get this matter reconsidered'.[13]

When Canterbury Convocation met in February 1904, Randall Davidson insisted on just such a reconsideration. He and others deplored the haste with which the question of the women's franchise had been decided, and the Archbishop admitted that his request for a reconsideration of the July decision was prompted by pressure from advocates of the women's cause. Again, as at the 1903 Church Congress, Gore regretted what he described as the 'positively and definitely retrograde step' of utterly excluding women from the Church franchise, and he warned against alienating women workers whose claim was 'of the gravest and widest kind'. E. S. Talbot, bishop of Rochester, supported Gore and explicitly drew the parallel between the movement for laymen's rights and the women's cause in the Church, urging churchmen 'to do more justice to the fundamental principle of the equality before God of male and female'. Unless the Church paid due attention to that principle, women might be tempted to insist on its indiscriminate application, demanding admission to the priesthood, seeking even to alter 'the condition under which the seat which his Grace now occupied was held'.[14]

After vigorous debate in both Houses, Convocation decided on 4 February to ask the first meeting of the Representative Church Council to reconsider the complete exclusion of women as electors. When that Council met on 8 July 1904, Davidson, Gore, and their allies (notably two prominent ecclesiastical lawyers, Sir Lewis Dibdin and P. V. Smith) persuaded a majority of delegates to request that a committee be appointed to devise an extension of the lay franchise 'so as not wholly to exclude women'.[15]

The committee, chaired by Bishop Herbert Ryle of Winchester, included Gore, Talbot, and other advocates of

[13] CCR (1903) 123–4, 127.   [14] CC (1904), 35, 11–12, 13–14.
[15] RCC (1904), 42.

the women's franchise as well as stalwart opponents such as Henry Wace, dean of Canterbury, J. L. Darby, dean of Chester, and two members of the Cecil family, Lord Salisbury, son of the former Prime Minister, and Lord Hugh. The committee spent more than a year on this and other constitutional problems; when it reported in November 1905, it proposed a double standard for the initial franchise very like that originally brought forward in 1903. Whereas all authentic churchmen would be qualified to vote for parochial lay representatives, only church-women who were 'entitled by ownership or occupation to vote as a vestry of the parish' received the franchise. [16]

This was somewhat unenthusiastically introduced by Bishop Gore to a thinly attended meeting of the Representative Church Council on 1 December 1905. He explained that it 'practically meant that women who would be entitled to the vote in municipal affairs should also be entitled to vote in ecclesiastical affairs', and he admitted that this was as much as could be achieved 'in present conditions'. In fact it was approved by the Council after very little debate.

This reluctant concession gained women very little power. Early in 1905, while the Ryle committee was still deliberating, the *Guardian* argued that women should have the initial franchise without restrictions, 'on an equal footing with men'. Even such a relatively liberal arrangement would have given women small political might. Assuming the numerical superiority of women voters in parish elections, the *Guardian* (8 February 1905) assured its readers that 'the balance will always be redressed, because the most they can do will be to vote for men who will vote for other men who will elect the Lay House. Moreover the other two Houses of the Representative Church Council will consist of men chosen by men.' As the property qualification further limited the number of women voters in the initial elections, it is hardly suprising that churchwomen viewed the franchise of 1905 as less

[16] *Guardian*, 8 Nov. 1905. Henry Wace (1836–1924) was dean of Canterbury from 1903 and formerly principal of King's College, London. He is described in the *DNB* as 'a strong partisan', and 'an outspoken opponent of innovation'. J. L. Darby, an Irishman, was dean of Chester from 1886.

than excitingly democratic. Nevertheless, it remained the
basis of women's participation in the government of the
Church of England until 1914.[17]

Within the Representative Church Council itself neither
the female franchise nor women's representation at any
level of Church council was seriously debated again until
1911, when Charles Gore (by then bishop of Oxford) again
took up their cause. On 22 November he persuaded the
Council to agree that 'it is desirable that a Committee be
appointed to consider afresh the question of the Franchise
of Women in the election of representatives of the laity in
Ruri-decanal and Diocesan Conferences, and consequently
in the House of Laymen'.[18] The result of that committee's
work was scrutinized by yet another committee, chaired
by the bishop of Southwell, Edwyn Hoskyns, which was
reviewing the whole range of problems connected with lay
representation. In its report to the Representative Church
Council on 9 July 1914, Hoskyns's committee recommended
not only that 'women be admitted to the parochial lay
franchise on the same terms as men', but also that women
be permitted to serve as representatives on parochial
councils, although to a maximum of one-third of the available places on each council. In the course of debate, the
numerical limitation was removed, and women were
declared eligible for all of the available lay seats on each
local council. They remained barred from ruri-decanal,
diocesan, and central councils.[19]

These concessions, modest as they appeared to feminists
in 1914, were won in the teeth of fierce opposition within
the Representative Church Council. Those who fought the
women's battle in debate stressed their fear that able and
politically conscious women were rapidly becoming alien-
ated from the Church. If churchmen 'thwarted the desire
of women to work with them upon the Councils of the
Church', Bishop Hoskyns was certain that they would

[17] *Church Times*, 1 Dec. 1905.

[18] *Guardian*, 24 Nov. 1911. Under the 1905 arrangement, in some dioceses
parochial councils elected delegates to ruri-decanal conferences which, in turn,
elected delegates to diocesan conferences. In other dioceses the deanery step
was omitted.

[19] RCC (1914), 25, 63–4.

'drive a great many of their best women out of the life of their Church and out of Church work into social organisations, and into political work'. He was supported in this view by Cosmo Gordon Lang, Archbishop of York, and by Bishop Winnington-Ingram of London, who said that the Council could not deliver 'a greater blow to the Church' than to bar women's participation in its political life. 'They were face to face . . . with a new thing in the world. The women were waking up to knowing things that they never knew before.'[20]

While the Church advanced with such extreme caution to expand women's role in its councils, the movement for women's parliamentary suffrage moved to the centre of the British political stage, gaining particular notoriety when the Women's Social and Political Union, the 'suffragettes', adopted militant tactics. There were many ardent Anglicans in suffragist ranks, including not only well-known activists, such as Maude Royden and Edith Picton-Turbervill, but also Louise Creighton, whose leading role in women's Church organizations was matched by her national prominence in secular bodies and government agencies. Many of these ladies belonged to the Church League for Women's Suffrage, founded in 1909 by the Revd Claude Hinscliff, who continued for many years as its secretary.[21] Although the first aim of the League was to 'secure for women the Parliamentary vote as it is or may be granted to men', and to do so by non-militant means, it also sought to draw out what its founder called 'the deep religious significance of the women's movement'.[22] Special celebrations of the Eucharist were held for suffragists and meetings were devoted to discussion of the spiritual dimension of the cause. In August 1912 the CLWS had more than 3,000 members, and by April 1914 this had increased to 'over 5,000 churchmen and churchwomen' whose primary commitment to the parliamentary cause still left some energy to lobby for

[20] RCC (1914), 20, 42.
[21] Claude Hinscliff to Archbishop Davidson, 5 Aug. 1912, Davidson Papers, W16, Lambeth Palace Library.
[22] Claude Hinscliff to Archbishop Davidson, 3 May 1912, Davidson Papers, W16, Lambeth Palace Library.

women's rights to elect and serve on Church councils. 'In Church matters', wrote CLWS member A. Laura Hills to the *Guardian* on 23 August 1912,

> where women are notoriously the largest givers and keenest workers the injustice of no representation is especially great, as they have no voice in Convocation, Houses of Laymen, or Ruri-decanal conferences. They are not even considered persons according to the S.P.G. charter . . . It behoves all women to work together to remove such anomalies.[23]

Archbishop Davidson, who was privately a passive suffragist in the parliamentary campaign, had considerable difficulty maintaining his customary noncommittal public stance as the women's struggle intensified. Between 1908 and 1914 militants put pressure on Davidson, particularly between January and September 1914, in connection with the effects of forcible feeding on imprisoned women under the notorious 'Cat and Mouse Act'. Those who wrote to him at this time condemned him for failing to rescue, or even to pray for, the brave persecuted suffragettes, and damned him for toadying to a heartless government. He was unjustly accused of ill-treating Annie Kenney, a suffragette who was arrested in Lambeth Palace after she refused to leave.[24] One group which took a particularly harsh line with the archbishop was the Suffragist Church-women's Protest Committee, whose secretary, Mrs Alice Kidd, condemned the 'servile attitude of the Heads of the Church towards an unjust and irresponsible government'. In October of that year, two months after the outbreak of the First World War, the Protest Committee sent the arch-bishop a letter, signed by forty-eight women, which began, 'We, the undersigned women, members of the Church of England, do hereby protest against the attitude of the Church towards the Woman's Movement for

---

[23] Elizabeth Metzler to Archbishop Davidson, 9 Mar. 1912, Davidson Papers, W16; *Guardian*, 1 Dec. 1909, letter from Elizabeth Hallowes; *Guardian*, 20 Dec. 1912; Hinscliff to Davidson, 5 Aug. 1912, Davidson Papers, W16; Susan Villiars to Archbishop Davidson, 3 Aug. 1914, Davidson Papers, papers on Women's Suffrage, 1908–14.

[24] G. K. A. Bell, *Randall Davidson, Archbishop of Canterbury* (London, 1952), 668–9; Davidson Papers, Women's Suffrage, 1908–14, *passim*.

reform, and towards her claim for enfranchisement, both in Church and State.'[25]

The campaign for the parliamentary suffrage thus reinforced the Church cause. Churchmen also experienced pressure directly on the ecclesiastical issue. Emma Paget, wife of the bishop of Stepney, went about talking to groups on the subject of women's representation in councils; in March 1914 she wrote to the archbishop for guidance and recommended that he push the matter forward.[26] Davidson, in turn, urged the bishop of Southwell to speed up the work of his committee on lay representation in the Representative Church Council. Long before that committee's report was accepted in the autumn of 1914, the Church press carried letters and articles pointing out both the expediency and the justice of a larger role for women in Church affairs. One such was that from 'Cornelia' in the *Guardian* of 1 December 1909. This writer deplored 'the depreciation of women's work and total ignoring of their status in the Church', and thought that 'it speaks volumes for the earnestness and devotion of the faithful daughters of the Church that in spite of almost universal neglect of their interests by the clergy, and the determined ignoring of their claims to recognition on her governing bodies, they still remain loyal'. On 5 January 1912 another *Guardian* correspondent, a member of the CLWS, described an African native congregation in which the women were included in decision making. 'This infant Church evidently recognises the right and necessity of women to express officially an opinion on religious and social life—a right doubtfully debated for English Churchwomen after centuries of Christianity.'

In 1915 the Church League for Women's Suffrage deliberately concentrated its efforts on the campaign to gain for women the full rights of laity in the Church, including equal political rights on Church councils. In a petition to the Representative Church Council the League protested,

[25] Alice Kidd to Archbishop Davidson, 14 June and 29 October 1914, Davidson Papers, Women's Suffrage, 1908–14.

[26] Emma Paget to Archbishop Davidson, Mar. 1914, Davidson Papers, W16. See also letters in the *Guardian*, 3 Feb. 1911 and *Guardian*, 31 Jan., 27 June 1913.

1. That the exclusion of women from the Ruri-decanal and
Diocesan Conferences and from the Representative Church
Council is an infraction of that spiritual equality of the sexes
which is a fundamental principle of the Christian faith. 2. That it
forbids the direct expression in these assemblies of women's
views upon questions . . . upon all of which women claim the
right to be heard, and upon some of which they can almost claim a
monopoly of first-hand knowledge. 3. That the authority of the
decisions of such assemblies is thereby weakened. 4. That a
stumbling-block is thereby placed in the path of many women
who regard their exclusion, deliberately decreed, as an infringe-
ment of their spiritual status . . . 5. That all women are thereby
deprived of the stimulus that comes from the sense of equal
opportunity and responsibility for both sexes alike.[27]

Some conservative-minded churchmen expressed alarm
that Church feminists (Maude Royden among them) were
taking the opportunity of wartime conditions to launch an
agitation for the ordination of women to the priesthood,
and, as we have seen, in 1916 a controversy developed
about the participation of women as preachers and
speakers in the National Mission.[28] In these ways women's
place in the ministry of word and sacraments became associated with the question of their rights in the councils of
the Church during the war years. It was an association
which anti-feminist churchmen thought as inevitable as it
was unpleasant, and one which prudent Church feminists
tried to play down.

Feminist agitation was not the only 'pressure from
without' felt by Church leaders on the subject of the
women's franchise and their place on Church councils.
The non-statutory character of all ecclesiastical assemblies
containing laymen, and the absence of any national
authority in the Church, resulted in a lack of uniformity
and undisciplined variety of practice, carrying the threat of
chaos. It is clear that some voluntary parish councils did

[27] *Guardian*, 25 March 1915.
[28] See the *Guardian*, 31 Mar. 1915, letter from 'X'. *Guardian*, 20 July 1916, letter
from Athelstan Riley; see the correspondence that follows continually up to
31 Aug. 1916. See also Archbishop Davidson to Athelstan Riley, 11 Aug. 1916,
Davidson Papers, Rll.

have women members despite the actions of Convocation in 1898 and of the Representative Church Council later. Sir Lewis Dibdin was alarmed to discover in 1909 that the diocese of Canterbury admitted 'women voters on the same level as men'. 'It was obvious', he thought, 'that they could not have one rule for female representation in one diocese and a different rule in another.' In the diocese of Rochester all churchwardens could be members of ruri-decanal conferences, and were also ex-officio members of the diocesan conferences; in that diocese women could occupy positions unattainable by their sisters in other parts of the Church. By 1913 the situation in Sodor and Man was even looser; women could vote for and be elected to the diocesan conference. According to one resident, 'There are at present three who have been so elected. One of them some time ago read a valuable paper before the Conference on "Church Music" and another gave a paper on "Sunday-School Work".'[29]

The pressure of feminists and the threat of disorder were factors in the modest concessions to women incorporated in the alteration of the lay franchise in July 1914. By that time, however, Church feminists were unlikely to be content with the concessions offered in that revision: the initial franchise and representation at the parish level only.

The year 1917 was critical both for the cause of Church self-government and for that of the Church suffragists. In November the Representative Church Council considered the *Report of the Archbishops' Committee on Church and State*, published in July 1916, a product of deliberations begun in 1913. Its recommendations for establishing a statutory system of Church self-government, modelled on the Representative Church Council, had been public for over a year. Archbishop Davidson's inaction during that year, his expressed unwillingness to proceed with Church reform in war-time, and the conservatism of the Committee's report on the woman issue, stirred a group of impatient clergy and laity to action. Inspired by H. R. L. Sheppard, led

[29] *Guardian*, 24 Nov. 1911, speech of Earl Nelson; *Guardian*, 14 July 1909, speech of Lewis Dibdin; *Guardian*, 4, 11 July 1913, letters from H. W. Johnston and Ernest B. Savage.

by William Temple, the Life and Liberty movement was formed in March 1917.[30] This 'ginger group' (which included both Louise Creighton and Maude Royden from the beginning) sought Church self-government immediately as a means to further Church reform later. Among its earliest productions was a pamphlet listing several 'scandals'; one of these was 'that there should be no place for women in the councils of the church'.[31]

When the Representative Church Council met in November 1917 to deal with the Archbishops' Committee's *Report*, it felt not only the full weight of the Life and Liberty campaign but also firm pressure from the Central Committee of Women's Church Work, a semi-official body made up of women from every diocese and many voluntary women's societies in the Church of England, chaired by Archbishop Davidson's wife. Encouraged by Louise Creighton (the vice-chairman), the Central Committee asked the Representative Church Council for its assurance that 'women should be eligible for election to the Diocesan Conferences and to the proposed Church Council as well as to the Parochial Councils, and further that they be granted in all administrative matters the same rights as other members of the laity'.[32]

Not for two more years did women achieve complete equality of opportunity in the councils of the Church. In the meantime, the *Report of the Archbishops' Committee on Church and State* was examined during most of 1918 by a very large Committee of the Representative Church Council (known as the 'Grand Committee'); in October it recommended widening considerably the scope of women's participation by allowing them to sit on ruri-decanal and diocesan conferences as well as on parochial councils. On the proposed national council, however, it maintained that only men should serve.[33] This final block

[30] F. A. Iremonger, *William Temple, Archbishop of Canterbury: His Life and Letters* (London, 1948), 220 ff.

[31] Carolyn Scott, *Dick Sheppard: A Biography* (London, 1977), 93.

[32] Central Committee of Women's Church Work, Minutes, 1909–19, 23 Oct. 1917, Minute Book 178, Church House Archives, London.

[33] *Report of the Committee of the Representative Church Council on the Report of the Archbishops' Committee on Church and State* (London, 1918), 15.

to equality was swept away by the Representative Church Council on 26 February 1919 on a motion by Bishop Kempthorne of Lichfield, seconded by William Temple. No doubt the submissions of Gore and other Church suffragists over the years had some influence on this result. No doubt, too, the Council responded to pressure from without, exerted by churchwomen themselves and by their allies in Life and Liberty. In the end, however, it was the example of the Parliamentary Reform Act of 1918 which carried the day. 'It would be an anomaly', said Kempthorne, 'that women should be considered eligible for the Parliament of the nation and not be eligible for the Representative Assembly of the Church.'[34] The enabling bill, providing for Church self-government, and allowing full lay rights for churchwomen in that government, passed through both Houses of Parliament in the last half of 1919. As the Church of England Assembly (Powers) Act, it received royal assent on 23 December.[35]

The National Assembly of the Church of England met for the first time in the following summer. Its members numbered 646, of whom 357 represented the laity; forty lay representatives were women.[36] Among those forty were at least two, Louise Creighton and Maude Royden, whose contributions to the women's cause had been outstanding, and who continued throughout the 1920s to be leaders of Church feminism. Although the Assembly never became a female preserve, the churchwomen did not shun their new opportunity. According to Charles Gore's biographer, between 1920 and 1935 'nearly ten times as many women . . . attained membership of the Church Assembly as . . . succeeded in entering the mother of Parliaments'.

There is no doubt, however, that churchwomen played an important role in the suffrage campaign, as well as in missions, in their efforts to gain power in the Church in the early twentieth century, particularly through the Church League for Women's Suffrage which published a

[34] *Guardian*, 6 Mar. 1919.   [35] Smith, *Church Self-Government*, p. 20.
[36] *National Assembly of the Church of England: Report of Proceedings, 1920* (London, 1921), 6.

'Monthly Paper' between 1912 and 1917.[37] The whole question of whether or not the bishops and archbishops were in general support of the CLWS or in fact saw it as a separate society remained unclear. Despite the insistence of members and leaders that the League was perfectly innocent of political aims, the *Standard* of 25 September 1913 remarked; '[since] no fewer than six members of the elected committee, including the chairman, are subscribers to the Women's Social and Political Union, a grave doubt must arise as to the real character of this outwardly respectable society'.[38]

The CLWS *was* an organization of the Church and indeed can be seen as the left wing of the Church. In 1917 it held a number of conferences; the first, in February, marked the organization as 'a starting point for those who wished to make the study of the Women's Movement from a Christian standpoint an outcome of the work of the National Mission'. According to the *Guardian* for 3 January 1918 the name was changed from CLWS to the League for the Church Militant in November 1917. The Manchester branch of the CLWS, however, was dissolved and became known in part as the Manchester League for Women's Service. Those who joined the new League declared,

> this step was forced upon us by an inability to accept the full programme of the League of the Church Militant. While realising that the question of the admission of women to the priesthood will have to be faced sooner or later, we are unwilling to imperil the success of efforts for urgent reform by committing the League to either side of this question. Our sole objects are to educate Church women in the responsibilities of citizenship and to secure the fullest opportunities of service for women in the Church and State.[39]

There is no doubt that a great deal of political work by the more advanced members of the women's organizations of the Church was funnelled through the CLWS and the

---

[37] The League existed from 1909 until 1919, when it became the League of the Church Militant.

[38] *Standard*, 25 Sept. 1913; *Southampton Daily Echo*, 26 Sept. 1913.

[39] *Commonwealth*, Mar. 1917, 90; *Guardian*, 20 Nov. 1919, letters from Canon Peter Green, Revd. R. C. Parsons.

LCM. In 1920 a report on the *Ministry of Women* announced that 'this society is the only one which, in addition to pressing for equalisation of opportunities as between the sexes, has laid emphasis on the primary importance of effecting this equalisation in the ministries of the Anglican Church'. These were decidedly political aims, and those who worked for them were decidely political people.

A number of meetings were held in the early 1920s by the LCM, many of them presided over by Maude Royden. At one, the following resolution was passed: 'that this meeting holds that sex should be no disqualification for admission to any of the lay ministries of the Church'. On 30 March 1921 the *Daily News* announced that Maude Royden's preaching on Good Friday

has strengthened the Movement growing in the Anglican Church for establishment of equal rights for women and men. This is shown, says Miss Gorben, of the League of the Church Militant, by the interest taken by the press in Miss Royden's service . . . The League of the Church Militant is at present preparing a memorial . . . The English Church Union is organizing a counter-petition in the hope of showing that a large number of church people are opposed to the ministry of women.

The journal *Church Militant* in January 1925 continued to battle against literalism in Scripture:

it is hard to win recognition for the truth that Christianity is definitely antagonistic to the view which regards woman as subordinate to man . . . to treat her as enjoying less than the full rights of human personality. Nor is this surprising. For partly through a misplaced reverence for the letter of Holy Scripture, partly through a blind adherence to ancient custom regardless of its source or content, the Church, which should be foremost to proclaim Christian principles—and scrupulous to honour it in the ordering of its own corporate life, has been in this matter of women most grievously to blame.

The end of the LCM came in 1928 with a public announcement: 'the general idea is that one major aim of the L.C.M.—equal franchise—is achieved and that advance is made towards the other, the ordination of women'. The *English Churchman* made a confident assertion: 'talk on women's service in the Church has advanced so rapidly that it is felt that ordination to the priesthood must inevitably follow in due time'.[40]

The CLWS and the LCM were not the only expressions of the suffrage movement within the Church of England. Before the war, Archbishop Davidson gave some support to women's suffrage, as indicated in Agnes Gardiner's correspondence in *The Times*. She pointed out that 'Both ' Archbishops Temple and Benson expressed themselves in favour of the proposal.' Archbishop Davidson was her main supporter. Although remaining cautious as time moved on, he indicated in a letter of 19 October 1910 to A. W. Chapman that he supported the movement but had 'kept outside the controversy altogether . . . because I have already far too many things in hand . . .'

In 1911 and 1912 a good deal of emphasis was placed on the religious aspect of the suffrage movement. From time to time there were special services for suffragists, for example, Percy Dearmer's at St Mary the Virgin, Primrose Hill, in 1912. One woman suffragist claimed that 'nothing could better indicate the seriousness of purpose among women suffragists than this celebration of the Eucharist, at which this priest, server and congregation were all members of various suffrage societies'. Mrs Creighton also helped align the National Council of Women behind women's suffrage at this time. In 1912 in *The Religious Aspect*, Bishop Gore remarked, 'with regard to a good many parts of the industrial life of the country and in the educational life of the country . . . it has been possible that woman's true place should be ignored and her interests overlooked only because the legislation of the country represented exclusively the male point of view'.[41]

[40] *The Ministry of Women: A Report by a Committee Appointed by the Archbishop of Canterbury* (London, 1920), 3; *English Churchman*, 9 Aug. 1928; *Women's Leader and Common Cause*, 10 Aug. 1928.

[41] Letters to Archbishop Davidson from Miss Agnes Gardiner, 5 Feb. 1907, Davidson Papers, Women's Suffrage, 1908–14; *Church Times*, 2 Dec. 1910, letter from F. Sherwell Cooper; letter from Elizabeth Metzler, 9 Mar. 1912, Davidson Papers, W16. Bishop Gore, *The Religious Aspect* (London, 1912), 32.

In pre-war years the opponents of suffragette militancy in the Bishops' Meeting complained that the CLWS was a militant cover-up.

One of the most deplorable features of this campaign of violence and crisis now being waged by the ruthless women who glory in the name of militant suffragettes is the encouragement they have received from certain Ministers and professed members of the Anglican Church. The C.L.W.S. has the Bishop of London as President; vice-presidents include the Bishop of Hereford, a Dean, two Archdeacons, two Canons and other churchmen and churchwomen of light and leading.[42]

Certainly, in the long struggle for·women's political recognition, some Anglican women and some Anglican men had played their part.

[42] *The Church League for Women's Suffrage and the Militants*, printed pamphlet in Davidson Papers, Women's Suffrage, 1908–14.

6

The Last Barrier:
Pastors and Preachers

THE tendency for amateur, paid, and professional Victorian women church workers to seek some form of training accelerated during the first decade of the twentieth century, and by 1917 the *Guardian* thought 'training' had become a catchword of the era. 'Everybody seems to be anxious to train everybody else, and hardly a month passes but the syllabus of some new training scheme is thrust before the notice of the public.[1] During the ten years or so before the World War a number of schemes and institutions appeared to prepare such women workers; all such ventures were small, and all were independent. They were without common standards and lacked any form of official Church recognition. After the war an effort was made to centralize the organization of women's full-time, paid pastoral work, to set common standards of training, and to examine and approve training centres; there was a continuing movement to provide the worker with a measure of institutional authorization and to assure her of adequate pay and decent conditions of employment. It was in the 1920s that the lay parish woman worker developed some of the characteristics of a professional person, even though she continued to lack access to real pastoral power (which was reserved to the parish priest) and was denied any share at all in the other charter elements of the clerical professional life.

Late in 1913, Emma Paget, wife of the bishop of Stepney and a leading proponent of expanding the role of women in ecclesiastical life, said 'more was being done than was generally known' to prepare women for church work. She

Part of this chapter is taken from Brian Heeney, 'Women's Struggle for Professional Work and Status in the Church of England, 1900–1930', *Historical Journal*, 26 (1983), 329–47, reproduced by kind permission of the editorial board of the journal.

spoke of sixteen 'training homes' in which 'educated women' could be trained, as well as of several settlements which offered similar facilities. Unfortunately none of the so-called 'homes' offered an agreed curriculum or conformed to an independent and common standard set by a recognized authority. Women who had completed the course at a training home could begin work without benefit of episcopal authority, provided they could find willing parishes with funds to make up their wholly unregulated stipends.[2]

Many criticisms of the arrangements for recruiting and training church workers were made over the next few years. Several of the training centres were operated by deaconesses and by religious orders; it was alleged that these failed to prepare women for life and work in the real world, or to deal with the needs and aspirations of modern women. Workers, argued the critics, ought not to be trained only to serve the clergy, to cater for existing clerical wants; rather 'they must aim at making the clergy want other things'. Criticism was voiced concerning the inadequacy of the academic standards of the training centres and their incapacity to extend their curriculum to include such new subjects as social work. William Temple took up the cause in the midst of the war, pressing for an official 'church training college, with a high standard of efficiency, preparing women for church work, for general social work, and perhaps for foreign mission work'.[3]

The idea of a central church training college for women, although it was much discussed during the last years of the war, came to nothing. However, exactly one month after the armistice the first meeting was held of the 'Training Committee' which, in July 1919, was to become the Inter-Diocesan Committee for Women's Work. At first designed merely to co-ordinate women's work in the metropolitan dioceses of London and Southwark, it soon expanded and added many other dioceses during the 1920s as more and more appointed diocesan boards of women's work.[4]

[1] *Guardian*, 5 July 1917.   [2] *Guardian*, 5 Dec. 1913.
[3] *Guardian*, 25 June 1914; 7 Dec. 1916; Temple, 'Co-operation in Social Work' in Bardsley (ed.), *Women and Church Work*, p. 36.
[4] Minute Book 187 (Training Committee, 1919–20), Church House Archives,

From the very beginning, the Inter-Diocesan Committee set about three tasks: to establish a 'common standard of requirements . . . for recognition in various branches of church work'; to 'test the qualifications of candidates submitted to it through Diocesan boards'; and to 'inspect recognised Training Centres'. Right at the beginning the Committee considered the sort of work for which it was testing candidates. Recognition was to be provided to specialized workers in teaching, rescue, and social work, and to those showing proof of training in both theological and social work. Examinations were provided in three areas: 'I. Theological Study; II. The Science and Methods of Teaching; III. Social Study, including special subjects, e.g. health and welfare work, methods of relief, rescue work among girls.' In 1930 the Inter-Diocesan Committee became a part of the Central Council for Women's Church Work, established not only to supervise training, but also to study problems 'connected with pay, status, conditions of work, the supply of workers and the demand for them'.[5]

At the time of the Inter-Diocesan Committee's dissolution, it had issued some 700 certificates to women church workers, who thereby gained a measure of professional recognition not available to churchwomen before 1919. It was, however, very limited recognition. There was still no compulsion on bishops to require inter-diocesan certificates from women seeking employment as church workers in the parishes of their dioceses. Nor can it be said that women themselves gained a significant measure of control over the nascent profession of parish worker. They continued to act wholly under the direction of males in both parish and diocesan contexts and they

London; *Church of England Year-book* (1921–30). By 1930, twenty-three dioceses had established councils or boards of women's work; Lambeth Conference Proceedings (hereafter LC), 11 July 1930, LC 1930, cxlvi, p. 452, 11 July (Lambeth Palace Archives).

[5] *Church of England Year-book* (1921), p. 238; Minute Book 187, Church House Archives, London. By 1930, four examination fields were offered: theology, pastoral work, social work, and educational work; Central Council of Women's Church Work, Minute Book 180, Church House Archives, London; *Church of England Year-book* (1931), pp. 483–4.

could not themselves aspire to the principal supervisory positions of priest or bishop. Furthermore, on the Inter-Diocesan Committee and its successor, the Central Council for Women's Church Work (which might have become a type of professional self-regulating body), men remained very powerful, although not actually numerically dominant.[6]

In the 1930s the Central Council for Women's Church Work continued to press its standards on training colleges and bishops alike, apparently with growing success. An intriguing little book, *Pastoralia for Women*, published in 1934 and edited by H. S. Marshall, a member of the Central Council, included several essays which outlined a large range of opportunities for properly-trained women in church-connected social work, as teachers, parochial visitors, and youth workers, as well as in the world of evangelization and in religious drama. The last two represent a small invasion of the second part of the clerical charter role, that of preaching; but all the other subjects are rightly included under the heading of pastoral care. The bishop of Southwell (Henry Mosley) in his Introduction, and H. S. Marshall in his Epilogue, both emphasized the special place of the properly-trained woman parish worker. She was not to be thought of as a substitute curate, but as one whose particular contribution was made both by reason of her training and also 'by reason of her sex . . . Her responsibility and the responsibility of the clergy are different in kind [but] there is no question of less or more.[7]

The trouble was that the reality of the woman worker's subordination was all too evident in her pay and her status on the parish staff. At the Lambeth Conference of 1930 the bishops stated their wish 'to emphasise that all paid workers should receive an adequate stipend together with a place in a recognised pension scheme, and work under a

---

[6] On the Inter-Diocesan Committee in 1921 there were thirteen men and eighteen women; all the men were clergymen, and a bishop was chairman. A bishop was chairman of the new Council after 1930. See Minute Books 187 and 180, Church House Archives, London.

[7] Henry Mosley, Introduction to *Pastoralia for Women*, H. S. Marshall (ed.) (London, 1934), 8.

formal agreement which specifies terms of employment, including time for study and provision for holidays'.[8] Despite these episcopal hopes, it is clear that adequate pay and equality of status remained two great unfulfilled aspirations of women workers well into the mid-1930s. In his handbook *A Parson's Job*, Leslie Hunter stated flatly that 'the Church does not pay women-workers an adequate wage and is living too complacently on their sense of vocation'. He went on,

A young deacon, uplifted by the feel of a collar turned back to front is liable to think he can teach a woman experienced in parish work or trained in Sunday School organization her job. He has to learn that such is the inadequacy of his training that she can in many ways teach him his. His vicar has to help him learn that lesson by giving a trained women a place on the staff comparable to that of the men, and allowing her scope for initiative in her special work in the parish.[9]

The arrogance of the young deacon was as understandable as it was disagreeable. He knew after all that he had access to the fullness of his chosen profession, that he could respond to his vocation up to the limits of his ability and strength. He also knew that his colleague, the woman parochial church worker, was stymied in her vocational response, in her professional fulfilment, by her sex. She was severely limited in her Christian ministry by her permanent lay status (or by the dubious status of the deaconess); worse than that, even her lay function was compromised by her sex.

If access to a more-or-less professional role in pastoral care was difficult for women, their efforts to participate professionally in the liturgical and homiletic life of the Church of England proved far more exasperating. By the twentieth century the clergy no longer had a monopoly on preaching, nor on the leadership of public worship; these functions had been opened to authorized laymen, and equality of opportunity with such men was the first object of those laywomen who wished for a public ministry which went beyond Sunday School teaching and pastoral

8 *The Lambeth Conferences, 1867–1948* (London, 1948), 266.
9 L. S. Hunter, *A Parson's Job*, p. 142.

care. In some cases the absence of men at the front in the World War was a factor in allowing women to perform what had traditionally been male roles. Thus The *Church Times* on 15 December 1916 thought it was quite appropriate for women to lead the singing at services in wartime, provided they were not dressed up in surplice and cassock (as were men and boys) but ordinarily garbed, and not located in the chancel (as male choirs were) but 'placed with the people in the body of the church'. On 15 April 1917 the *Christian Commonwealth* reported that six women at the parish church of Bedford Park 'were elected sidesmen, and they now take up the collections and assist at the services exactly as the men did whom they replace'.

Such relatively minor incursions into traditional male domains do not seem to have aroused much controversy. Very different was the situation after the wife of a country parson wrote to the *Guardian* on 10 February 1916 asking why women could not read the lessons at regular church services 'in . . . villages where there is no man who could, or would, stand up and read the lessons'. There followed over a month of warm correspondence, much of it hostile on the ground that 'universal custom' forbade women to take such a public ecclesiastical role.

The first really heated controversy occurred later in 1916 and centred on the role of women in the National Mission of Repentance and Hope, planned by the archbishops to spark a wartime revival of English faith and religious practice. The council appointed to plan the Mission adopted a resolution which had been proposed by the ardent church feminist Maude Royden, 'to urge upon the bishops the importance of giving definite directions as to the best ways of using the services and receiving the message of women-speakers, whether in church or elsewhere'.[10] Many clergy and laymen were scandalized by this assumption that women would have an authorized place as speakers in church, and a row erupted focused in the columns of the Anglo-Catholic *Church Times*. Opposition to women speakers in church took several forms. It was claimed as evidence of a sinister

[10] The *Guardian*, 20 July 1916. Maude Royden, in addition to being a leading church feminist, was a prominent suffragist and editor of *Common Cause*.

'conspiracy', a 'feminist plot', the ultimate object of which was to open up the priesthood to women. Some took their stand firmly on a literal interpretation of some of St Paul's works, especially 1 Corinthians 14:34–5. These complaints constituted a considerable pressure on the bishop of London who had already presumed to authorize women preachers in the churches of his diocese during the Mission. The lobbyists were successful and Bishop Winnington-Ingram withdrew his permission in September 1916.[11]

The unwillingness of the bishop to sustain his permission to women preachers was regarded as a severe setback by feminists. In the face of this defeat some women (Maude Royden and Edith Picton-Turbervill were the most prominent) simply decided to break the rules, if possible in Anglican pulpits, if necessary in nonconformist ones. Maude Royden, while still remaining an Anglican, accepted, as we have already seen, and invitation to become assistant minister at the Congregationalist City Temple in 1917, subsequently and notoriously later preaching in an Anglican church each Good Friday. Edith Picton-Turbervill preached at the anniversary service of the parish of North Somercotes in Lincolnshire at the invitation of the rector and with the consent of Edward Lee Hicks, the diocesan bishop.[12] Once Royden and Picton-Turbervill had broken the ice a few others followed their lead. In 1924, for example, Lady Barrett preached at Bristol Cathedral, and four years later Beatrice Hankey, a person of remarkable and idiosyncratic spirituality, delivered a sermon at Liverpool Cathedral.[13]

[11] The opposition was also featured in the *Guardian*. The term 'conspiracy' was used by the prominent Anglo-Catholic layman, Athelstan Riley, in a letter to the *Guardian* on 20 July 1916. 'The feminist plot' is the title of an article in that paper on 10 Aug. 1916. *Guardian*, 10 Aug. 1916; *Church Times*, 15 Sept. 1916. Royden's move to the City Temple was described as 'a sort of ecclesiastical militancy' by a correspondent, Frances Eeles in a letter to Royden, dated 10 Mar. 1917; Royden Papers, No. 222, Fawcett Library, London. She was forbidden to preach on Good Friday at St Botolph's in London and actually spoke in an adjoining parish room instead; *Daily Chronicle*, 19 Apr. 1919. In 1921 she preached at the Good Friday service in the same church, 'ignoring the objection of the bishop of London'; *Daily Chronicle*, 26 Mar. 1921.

[12] *Guardian*, 26 June 1919; *Daily Mirror*, 1 June 1919. Edith Picton-Turbervill (1874–1958) was an officer of the YWCA and a suffragist as well as a church feminist. From 1929 to 1931 she was a Labour MP.

[13] Maude Royden, *The Church and Woman*, p. 146; Raven and Heath, *One Called Help*, p. 268.

While the militants took direct action, moderate church feminists tried to influence the Convocations of the Church of England and the bishops gathered at Lambeth from all over the Anglican communion in 1920. The first such lobby was the all-female Central Committee of Women's Church Work (whose chairman was the archbishop of Canterbury's wife, and which included several other bishops' wives and widows on its executive). On 23 October 1918 the Central Committee accepted a resolution that 'permission [be] given to women to speak at non-liturgical services . . . in consecrated buildings under a system of authoritative licence' and that 'in the present emergency caused by the absence of so many of the clergy at the front, the bishops be asked . . . to authorize duly qualified, trained and tested women to give addresses, to hold intercession services, read the lessons in church, and help . . . in other ways'.[14] After the war (which ended less than a month after the ladies' resolutions were passed) the English bishops were released from the Central Committee's second recommendation. However, in 1919 they arranged for a joint committee of bishops and other clergy to bring a report to the Convocation of Canterbury on women's role in the ministry. While carefully pointing out that 'the idea of women being ordained to the priesthood [is] . . . wholly contrary to the immemorial and consistent custom of the Catholic Church', the committee went on to state that

it should be allowed for women to speak and pray in consecrated buildings under regulations and conditions laid down by the bishop at services or meetings other than the liturgical services of the church, that is, the order of Holy Communion and Morning and Evening Prayer, together with the occasional offices.

This positive if unheroic statement was essentially the same as that adopted by the Lambeth Conference of bishops in the following year.[15] It was too strong,

14 Central Committee of Women's Church Work, Minute Book 178, Church House Archives, London.
15 *Guardian*, 17 July 1919; *The Six Lambeth Conferences, 1867–1920* (London, 1920), 41.

however, for most members of the lower house of the Canterbury Convocation. Debated continually from 1919 to 1922, it finally emerged in a weakened form: women's right to speak and lead prayers in consecrated buildings was 'normally' to be confined to congregations of women and children. [16]

The debates of Convocation in these years, and the episcopal discussions at Lambeth during the summer of 1920, contained many of the same arguments against women preachers as those expressed in the church press during the National Mission debate of 1916. Again a selection of St Paul's words on woman's place were trotted out and asserted as definitive. Again it was alleged that even a carefully limited opening of pulpit and chancel to laywomen would place the Church on a slippery slope, the end of which was a female priesthood. Once more the Church was warned that to allow women any part in public ministry within the church building was to threaten relations with Roman Catholic Christians. [17]

There were some new wrinkles too. Dr Sparrow Simpson made much of the 'principle of subordination' which he perceived clearly both in nature and in scripture. The bishop of Exeter (Gascoyne Cecil) insisted that women's participation in leading public worship would confuse spheres of human activity best kept separate: 'the religious instinct and the sexual instinct were too close to be allowed to be brought into close contact'. Finally, there appeared an argument which may well have had a larger place than actually shows in the public debates. When the dean of Canterbury, Henry Wace, observed that 'there were differences not only in the physical but in the psychical constitution of women which rendered the office of regular public preaching unsuitable for them', he was hinting at mysteries and myths of sexual difference which clearly worried many. [18]

The 1920 Lambeth Conference asked a well-known female physician, Dr Letitia Fairfield (also an active church

[16] CC (1922), 315.
[17] CC (1920), 30; (1919), 103; (1922), 229.
[18] CC (1920), 30; (1919), 101; (1920), 36.

feminist) to comment privately on the medical aspects of 'women and the lay ministries'. The document she produced is both a sharp rejection of alleged medical groups for excluding women from such ministries and a severe commentary on the debilitating myths surrounding menstruation. She observed that 'neither preaching nor serving [at the altar] is a harder task physically than district visiting or sunday school teaching or addressing congregations in church rooms or mission halls'. After reviewing and rejecting all sorts of alleged weaknesses in women, she concluded that the real reason for blocking women's ministry was a continuing, partly subconscious, belief in her 'ceremonial uncleanness'; superstitions about menstruation, she told the bishops, were of 'fundamental importance'. The Church's refusal to permit women to serve professionally at a level comparable to that attained in the great secular professions 'cannot be founded on a lack of spiritual worth . . . nor on mental quality . . . The difference, therefore, must be physical.' That physical cause, argued Fairfield, must be menstruation, and the primitive fancy that women's 'liability to periodic illness makes her permanently defiled by her sex in a sense that man is not'. It was this supposed 'defilement', she believed, that kept women out of the pulpit and chancel. [19] Dr Fairfield's view corresponded with Maude Royden's own experience. In her draft autobiography she wrote of the 'singularly nauseous quality' of the opposition to women preachers, an unpleasantness 'which exceeded anything I had met with in the fight for the vote'. It was assumed, if not actually stated, that the presence of a woman in pulpit or chancel would 'result in the desecration of the church', simply because of her sex and in spite of the highest spiritual qualities she might possess. [20]

Whatever the weight assigned individually to this and the other particular reasons put forward for excluding women from the pulpit and from lay service in the

[19] Letitia Fairfield, 'Women and Lay Ministries', LC 1920, cxxxvi, pp. 61–70 (Lambeth Palace Archives).
[20] 'Bid me Discourse', Royden Papers, No. 224, Fawcett Library, London.

sanctuary, when combined they proved to have much force. Despite the success of a few rebels (of whom Maude Royden was the most outstanding), despite the fact that a considerable number of women were theologically qualified to preach (since early in the century a few women had regularly passed special examinations established by the archbishop of Canterbury, chiefly to test teachers of religion), no serious progress had been made by 1930 towards the authorization of women preachers. In the course of a generally cheerful review of women's place in the Church of England in 1930, the bishop of Blackburn (Percy Mark Herbert) admitted to his fellow bishops at the Lambeth Conference of that year that 'there has been . . . very little advance in the matter of giving permission to women to speak in church'.[21]

If continuing restraints on women occupying Church of England pulpits barred them from sharing the commission to preach the Gospel, even more substantial barriers blocked women from the full liturgical ministry. Their sex rendered them ineligible for ordination to the priesthood, and only priests could celebrate Holy Communion and administer absolution. Priests also performed all the other functions of the charter role of the clerical profession; they were the regular pastors, the principal preachers, and the chief leaders of public worship in the Church of England. Consequently both advanced church feminists and their more entrenched opponents saw ordination to the priesthood as the key issue upon which women's place in the Church's ministry ultimately turned. It became the strategy both of radicals and of conservatives to make this point as sharply as possible. On the other hand, moderates on both sides were reluctant to focus on access to the priesthood; they preferred to seek compromises by which women could share liturgical (as well as homiletic and pastoral) functions and yet dodge the main issue. Moderates looked for a solution sufficiently liberal to answer the women's needs within the traditional framework of subordination to the male clergy.

Advanced church feminists first raised the matter of ordination to the priesthood in the church press a few

[21] LC 1930, cxlvi, p. 453, 11 July (Lambeth Palace Archives).

years before World War I. On 8 April 1910 one lady (disguised as 'a questioner') did so in a letter to the *Guardian*. She was supported by a number of correspondents who cited the manpower shortage in the ordained ministry, the proven ability of women as speakers, teachers, and parish visitors, and the ambivalence of St Paul on the position of women in the church. The alleged self-interest of male priests in monopolizing their profession was denounced. The apparently innocent 'questioner' also inspired shocked and spirited opposition: 'the universal custom of the church from the first, not to mention a sense of decency and propriety, apparently goes for nothing', wrote one clergyman, 'but surely a joke is intended', he added hopefully. Another referred to the idea as a 'wicked return to the ideals of heathenism' which would drive men away from both the ministry and congregations. A scriptural argument was produced which was to be used by opponents of women's ordination to the priesthood for over sixty years to come: that Jesus had chosen men as apostles, and in so doing defined the ordained ministry as a male preserve for all time. [22]

A small conference was planned by advocates of the ordination of women for August 1914; the planning group included not only such feminists as Maude Royden and Edith Picton-Turbervill, but also the well-known scholarly clergymen B. H. Streeter and Percy Dearmer. [23] This meeting was actually abandoned at the outbreak of war; but rumours about it, and revelations of the advanced opinions of its sponsors, led some to believe that feminists were actively plotting to introduce women to the priesthood.

By 1916 advocacy of the priesthood for women had become a recognized part of the church feminist cause, and its champions were recognized as the *avant-garde* of that cause. One such was Mary Morshead, a secondary schoolteacher in charge of the religious education of over

[22] *Guardian*, 8, 15 Apr., 6 May 1910.
[23] The list of prospective participants in this conference is contained (in handwriting) on the opening page of a book of newspaper cuttings included in the large collection of cuttings entitled 'Women and the Church' (Box IV) in the Fawcett Library, London.

300 girls, who felt a call to serve as her students' chaplain. She wrote to the *Guardian* on 23 November 1916,

There could hardly be a more important or responsible cure of souls. Churchmen hold and teach that for those who have the cure of souls there is provided that special grace of ordination. I ask for that grace. They offer me a diploma signed and given by the Archbishop . . . is this not an almost grimly humorous instance of the children asking for bread and being given a stone?

Miss Morshead's appeal drew much denunciation in subsequent *Guardian* correspondence. Indeed the next year or two saw something of a pamphlet war. The 'antis' were compelled to take the assault on the priesthood seriously, and they launched vigorous anti-feminist appeals, such as that by Arnold Pinchard, entitled *Women and the Priesthood* (1916). Pinchard placed much weight on familiar biblicist sexism: 'in Holy Scripture, God is always spoken of as if he were in the male sex'; 'when the everlasting son took human nature . . . he took *male* human nature'. He also argued that men and women had separate spheres of activity, that 'there is given to the male a certain superiority . . . priority of initiative and decision . . . a kind of final responsibility'. Priesthood, he believed, was an inherent part of this sphere of male superiority.[24]

No doubt it was this polarizing of extreme opinion that moved moderate feminists to urge in 1917 that the question of priesthood be put to one side, that more promising and less divisive aims be pursued. Louise Creighton actually thought that the admission of women to Holy Orders 'was . . . undesirable and at the present moment would be disastrous'. William Temple based his opposition on 'grounds of general expediency and not of fundamental principle', a view he was to retain as archbishop of York in 1930. Also in 1917, B. H. Streeter expressed the opinion that the issue should be 'indefinitely postponed . . . until the great majority of members of the church, both men and women, are convinced that it is desirable'.[25]

[24] Arnold Pinchard, *Women and the Priesthood* (London, 1916), pp. 4, 7, 8.
[25] B. H. Streeter and E. Picton-Turbervill, *Woman and the Church* (London, 1917), p. 100; *Guardian*, 22 Feb., 1 Nov. 1917; LC 1930, cxlvii, p. 69.

In the 1920s opinion on the ordination question hardened further. Both the Lambeth Conferences of 1920 and 1930 came out firmly against the ordination of women to the priesthood. The Archbishop of Canterbury's Commission on the Ministry of Women (whose report was published in 1920) concluded that 'the restriction of the ministry of the priesthood to men originated in a generation which was guided by the special gifts of the Holy Spirit'. Another official commission took much the same view in 1935, and also found itself unable 'to recommend the admission of women to the priesthood'.[26] The Convocation of Canterbury, which had such difficulty allowing women even to speak in church, never seriously considered the matter of women priests in the 1920s. On the other side, the small minority of enthusiasts for a female priesthood were concentrated in the League of the Church Militant. In June 1926 the League's periodical, the *Church Militant*, stated that 'the cause for which we stand uniquely by reason of our churchmanship is that of the openness to women of the ministry of the Word and Sacraments'.

Moderate advocates of the women's cause avoided the priesthood issue during the first thirty years of the century mainly because they thought it was hopeless, a pointless diversion from more attainable goals. Nevertheless, some moderates knew that women's full participation in the professional ministry of the Church must have a liturgical side as well as homiletic and pastoral dimensions. They hoped that this could be achieved through the development of the office of deaconess.

There had been slow progress in the provision of deaconesses within the Church of England, in the Bishops' Meeting of 21 June 1905, the bishop of Newcastle (Edgar Jacob) asked if there was any hope of a future report by the committee appointed by the Lambeth Conference of 1897. The archbishop of Canterbury explained that the first half of the report (that on communities) had been presented in 1898 and printed in 1901. The second half had been

---

[26] *The Ministry of Women: A Report by a Committee Appointed by . . . the Archbishop of Canterbury* (London, 1920), p. 5; *Archbishops' Commission on the Ministry of Women* (London, 1935), p. 9.

delayed by the deaths of Bishops Stubbs and Creighton and by other causes. On the whole, in view of some developments especially in America, he was not sorry for the delay which had taken place. He thought, however, that the committee might with advantage meet in the autumn. Even in 1914 deaconesses were not regarded as free priests, 'deaconesses in the Anglican Communion and body do not regard their Order as in any way whatever a step in the direction of the priesthood . . . I am anxious to prevent the idea becoming prevalent that existing deaconesses desire the priesthood.' A few years before, Deaconess Gilmore had made clear the subordination of the deaconess to the parish priest; she also believed deaconesses 'ought to be of mature age, in sound health, of good education, and if possible, of some means'. In the same year Deaconess Gilmore was appointed to create and define roles for deaconesses in the parish; these included visitation, teaching, care of sanctuary, and liaison with the parish officials.[27]

The rising sense of feminism in certain sections of the Church brought the issue of deaconesses to the fore. According to John Lee's leading article in the *Guardian* of 8 February 1917,

behind the speeches and the enthusiasm the central idea took form. The question of a Diaconate for men and for women is clear before us. There are many men and women available. Their services might be graded, much as the Bishops grade lay readers now. It has ceased to be a woman's question. It was never a question of women priests—even the question of women preachers is subsidiary. It is a demand for a thorough reconsideration of the present un-Catholic system of apprentice-deacons.

Frequently, deaconesses were more than mere substitute priests, 'why not allow deaconesses to take the evening services in churches?' A suburban vicar wrote to the *Daily Mirror* on 29 April 1918 that 'the duties of a deaconess are

[27] Bishops' Meeting, 21 June 1905, Lambeth; *Guardian*, 30 July 1914, letter from the Revd J. H. Browne, Warden of Rochester and Southwark Diocesan Deaconess Institution; Deaconess Isabella Gilmore, 'Women's Work in the Church', CC (1909).

similar to those of a layman, who can act for a clergyman in all capacities but those of pronouncing absolution or administering the sacrament . . . she can even baptise if there is no clergyman within call. She is often a skilled maternity and sick nurse.' The 1920 Lambeth Conference agreed with the bishop of Southwell when he said, 'I press that we should entrust deaconesses when ordained, with certain rights which are not given to the ordinary lay woman.'[28] The real question facing the bishops was, 'is the female diaconate a permanent office or order (as the male diaconate is) or is it (like the position of Church Warden) merely temporary?' The chairman of Canterbury Convocation believed that there is 'no forward graduation suggested here. It is merely that women should be admitted to one of the existing orders. The bishop of Durham told the Conference that the discussion of deaconesses

comes before us now in a new and very grave connection . . . the very important and very remarkable feminist movement . . . I would point out that an effective answer to the demand now being pressed by educated women is not the offer of a subordinate office such as that which is predicated in the diaconate but rather an open career which women of ability can pursue and in which they can express themselves fully and in which they can find the full satisfaction of their legitimate ambitions. The issue really is, as the Bishop of Ely very frankly stated: shall women be admitted to Holy Orders?[29]

The bishops at the Lambeth Conference seemed prepared to admit that the order of deaconesses was a real part of the ordained ministry, sharing in Holy Orders, in some sense the equal of the male diaconate. Whereas the bishops gave no encouragement to a female priesthood, they agreed to a resolution that 'The Order of Deaconesses is for women the one and only Order of the Ministry which has the stamp of Apostolic approval, and is for women the only Order of the Ministry which we can recommend that our branch of the catholic church should recognise and use.' They went on to recommend an authentic form of ordination

[28] John Lee, 'The Laywoman in the Church', *Guardian*, 8 Feb. 1917; LC 1920, cvii, p. 248, 29 July (Lambeth Palace Archives).
[29] LC 1920, cvii, p. 193, 29 July; ibid., cxli, p. 28 (Lambeth Palace Archives).

and to specify that deaconesses should 'in church . . . lead in prayer and, under licence of the Bishop . . . instruct and exhort the Congregation'.[30]

The problem was that the functions assigned to deaconesses did not include the distinctive duties of the male deacon: to assist with the chalice at Holy Communion and to read the Gospel. These exclusions were undoubtedly deliberate. Review of the actual debate at the Conference reveals, for example, the bishop of Ottawa's insistence that 'the ministry of the deaconess will be limited to ministry outside the altar rails' and the fears of some of his colleagues that a deaconess 'assisting in any shape or form in the administration of Holy Communion . . . will be regarded as a first step towards admitting women to the priesthood'. Failure to assign primary diaconal functions to deaconesses, fortified by such expressions of opinion, made nonsense of Archbishop Davidson's statement that Lambeth was recommending the admission of women to the regular diaconate.[31]

Confusion on this critical point (the relation between the office of deacon and that of deaconess) persisted throughout the 1920s and no doubt contributed to the decline in the number of English deaconesses from about 300 in 1920 to 216 in 1930.[32] As L. S. Hunter observed in *A Parson's Job*,

the result of starting the Order without defining its function has made ordination look rather ridiculous; while the absence of distinguishing functions may almost inevitably lead to a tendency to stress 'position' and 'precedence' and to create awkward relations between deaconesses and other women workers whose sense of vocation may be as strong as theirs and whose training and education may sometimes be better.[33]

In 1922 the Lambeth Lower House of Canterbury Convocation passed 'by large majorities' two amendments 'prohibiting deaconesses from reading Morning and Evening Prayer and the Litany and from leading in prayer and

---

[30] *The Six Lambeth Conferences, 1867–1920*, p. 40–1.
[31] LC 1920, cvii, pp. 178, 217, 236 (Lambeth Palace Archives). The bishop of Ottawa was John Charles Roper.
[32] LC 1930, cxlvii, p. 144 (Lambeth Palace Archives).
[33] Hunter, *A Parson's Job*, p. 142.

preaching at church services'. In 1923, £120 per annum was recognized as the minimum salary for a deaconess, but £150 was becoming the more usual amount. About 130 deaconesses were present at the Seventh Annual Conference in 1924 held at Church House, Westminster, including representatives from India, China, Jamaica, and Canada.[34]

In 1926 Bishop Temple of Manchester recognized that the Order of Deaconesses was

a true Order in the Church of England and it was necessary that a place be got for the work of women in the Church . . . He trusted that the full recognition of the Diaconate of women would lead to the coming forward of more women, especially women of ability and education, to be trained as deaconesses. His hope was that the Deaconess Movement would become the vanguard of the whole Movement for the enlargement and extension of the ministry of women in the Anglican Church.

In 1926 the *Church Militant* reported that

the L.C.M. Annual Council [9 March 1926] welcomes the formation of the Provincial Council for the Order of Deaconesses as a further official recogniton of the Ministry of Women in the Church and desires the Council to approach the authorities of the Church asking them to give an unequivocal ruling as to whether the Deaconess is or is not ordained to the Third Order of the Ministry.[35]

The 1930 Lambeth Conference added nothing to the duties of deaconesses as described ten years before. The matter of deaconesses assisting at Holy Communion was discussed, along with the possibility of their participation in the churching and burial offices. Such sharing in the ministry of deacons was rejected. The Conference Committee on Deaconesses explicitly stated that the deaconess was not a deacon at all but rather 'outside the historic Orders of the ministry . . . supplementary and complementary to them'.[36]

[34] *Manchester Guardian*, 7 July 1922; *Guardian*, 27 July 1923; 4 July 1924; *Manchester Guardian*, 18 June 1926.
[35] *Church Militant*, 1 Apr. 1926.
[36] LC 1930, cxlvii, pp. 138, 171; LC 1930, clxv (Subcommittee on Deaconesses), pp. 15, 34–5. .

The attempted revival of deaconesses as 'for women the one and only Order of the Ministry'[37] proved a great disappointment to those who hoped it might develop into an acceptable vehicle for the professional service of women within the ordained ministry of the Church of England, a means by which women might gain an acceptable share of the liturgical, homiletic, and pastoral charter role of the clerical profession. With her function ill-defined, denied even a listing in Crockford's *Clerical Directory*, the deaconess was relegated to a professional status very inferior to that of a clergyman, hardly distinguishable indeed from that of trained paid lay workers. It was a position which had not perceptibly improved by the mid-1970s.[38]

Whereas the first three decades of the century saw considerable expansion and development in the scope of women's work for the Church, the movement evidently stalled in the early 1930s, to regain momentum only with the renewal of militant feminism and the vigorous (but unsuccesful) drive for female ordination in the 1970s. By 1930 the activist, politically-conscious League of the Church Militant had disbanded; it was succeeded by the far less aggressive interdenominational Society for the Equal Ministry of Men and Women in the Church and by the Anglican Group for the Ordination of Women.[39] Despite the faithful lobbying of these pressure groups before and after World War II and the forceful actions of their successors on the contemporary scene, true sharing by women in the professional functions of pastoral care, preaching, and public worship in the Church of England remains to be achieved.

The major period of church feminism was basically that of the First World War and the ten years after it. In that

[37] LC 1920, Resolution 48; LC 1930, Resolution 67.

[38] LC 1930, cliv, pp. 150–1; Hunter, *A Parson's Job*, p. 142; Hugh Melinsky, *Patterns of Ministry* (London, 1974), 17.

[39] See Margaret J. Roxburgh, *Women's Work in the Church of England* (London, 1958). The interdenominational society changed its name to the Society for the Ministry of Women in the Church in 1957. The rhythm of church feminism in the twentieth century has corresponded remarkably to that of feminism generally according to Kate Millett's analysis in her *Sexual Politics* (New York, 1969); in both, 1930 marks the beginning of a resting phase, thirty years or so of non-militancy.

period one finds the question frequently raised and recognized as troublesome. For example the Revd W. C. Roberts wrote to the *Guardian* that although he 'will never himself desire to see women in the priesthood, he believed that his hesitations were emotional and not rational. He put all his scholarship and his judgement at the disposal of the little group of people who were beginning in 1913 to think and pray about the issues that were involved.' A conference was evidently revealed to the *Guardian* of 16 July 1914 by a Mr. M. W. Hill at Ripon Church Council Meeting in the previous week. A coterie of ladies planning a conference to discuss the question of the ordination of women to the priesthood came as no surprise to council, although 'not so novel as is commonly supposed, for not so many years ago it was advanced by a lady who wrote a letter to the *Guardian* on the subject'.[40]

Opposition to ladies' ordination was various and this chapter ends with a brief survey of its characterist manifestations. Mrs Creighton said in the *Guardian* of 22 February 1917, 'it would erect a hopeless barrier between the Church of England and the Roman Catholic and Orthodox Churches, and in such a matter it was essential that the whole Catholic Church should move together.' Mr A. C. MacGee, in opposing Maude Royden, said,

it would have been better to present one fundamental principle —one being sufficient—and invite Miss Royden to dispose of it. There is one such fundamental principle, and we doubt whether any other argument on the same side has much value. It is the principle that so great a change must not be made except by the common consent of the whole church.

No longer was sex considered a limitation or introduction to women's ordination. Hensley Henson, bishop-elect of Durham, said,

I submit that it will be found that in the long run that you cannot in your concessions to female demands stop short of the episcopate itself . . . you admit women to councils, and what security is there that in due course those councils will contain an over-

---

[40] W. C. Roberts in the *Guardian*, 8 Apr. 1910; Susan Miles, *Portrait of a Parson* [i.e. W. C. Roberts] (London, 1955), 37.

whelming majority of women? You have a very large majority of women among your communicants at this moment.

Henson went on to ask the Lambeth Conference on 8 July 1920,

can you really reasonably and rightly distinguish between the Ministry of the Word and the Ministry of the Sacrament? Nothing has astonished me more . . . than this faculty with which eminent ecclesiastics even bishops admit, as if it were an obvious proposition, that the Ministry of the Word should be granted to women, while they yet shrink with something like horror from the idea that the Ministry of the Sacrament should be granted to women. . . . I should myself . . . submit that the practical argument for the Ministry of the Sacraments being entrusted to women is a very strong one. Half, or something more than half, the human race is female.

In 1921 Mr MacGee numbered himself among the supporters of the feminist movement in the Lambeth Resolutions of 1920 when he argued that indeed

they are valued as a stepping stone to other things. The Chancel step . . . is merely a step towards the altar, which is the goal of all their ambitions . . . when the hour comes, for which this mistaken policy is preparing the way, all the restrictions and qualifications which at present adorn the Lambeth Resolution will be sent on a journey to Jupiter.

In 1921 in the CCR one speaker reminded the audience of 'grave psychological reasons for refusing to extend the ministry of women in the Church . . . there are certain qualities pre-eminently characteristic of women which in the strain and stress of public work are weakened and injured'. [41] In 1922 the English Church Union received over 54,000 protests from its membership of women and sent these to Archbishop Davidson. Many other Catholics would be appalled by women priests, wrote Alice Dewdney in the *Morning Post* of 31 March 1928. In some cases the opposition to a woman priesthood was biblically based, as in the letter from L. K. Wilson to the *Daily Express* on 16

[41] *Church Times*, 13 June 1919; LC 1920, cvi, pp. 50–1, 8 July, Bishop-Elect of Durham (Henson); ibid., pp. 51–2, 8 July (Lambeth Palace Archives); CCR (1921), McGee.

April 1928: 'this is not a matter of "logic" or sex equality: it is a principle for which we church people stand. We simply do not agree about it. Our Christian religion is founded on the doctrine of Christ and His Apostles. We cannot go against St. Paul's teachings.' There was opposition to women serving in the sanctuary. It was even unusual for women to take up the collection. Women servers were under suspicion; 'Bishop Temple of Manchester said he could see no reason "in principle" against women servers', but 'there are many considerations of expediency and . . . the question ought to be settled not by individual bishops for their own dioceses but by the church as a whole'. Men were alleged to be superior at distinctly priestly work, 'intellectual, sacramental and authoritative'.[42] Furthermore, the challenge in 1916 was treated as the ultimate point that motherhood would incapacitate women for the priesthood.

Maude Royden, on the other hand, outlined five reasons commonly given against the priesthood for women. They were: 1. subordination because of physical weakness; 2. taboo of uncleanness; 3. bearing children; 4. sexual attraction; 5. ecumenical considerations. In 1920 deaconesses were said to be pressing for the priesthood if they were allowed to assist at the communion for the sick in any way. Women were said to be incapable of priesthood as men are incapable of motherhood. A major argument against allowing women priests stemmed from traditionalism: 'nearly 2,000 years, the whole of its duration hitherto, the Church has had one rule. It has confined official ministry to men . . . no woman has ever ministered at the altars of Christiandom. No woman has yet been authorised as preacher in the Churches' official ministry. This is the Catholic custom, universal in East and West.'

Some argued that there was really a more responsible reason for women's ministry. 'Women . . . are drifting outside the influence of a church, which practically refuses to women any real share in its regular and recognised

---

[42] CC (1922), 191–2; *Daily Chronicle*, 3 Mar. 1922, letter from W. G. Roach; *Daily Chronicle*, 27 Feb. 1922, letter from 'FIAT LUX'; *Modern Churchman*, Nov. 1923, letter from J. R. Wilkinson; *Church Family Newspaper*, 10 Mar. 1922; *The Times*, 19 Nov. 1924.

138   *The Last Barrier: Pastors and Preachers*

ministry.' Such refusal demands a reaction. A dissenting minister gave the basic reason for women priests: 'woman's supreme function of motherhood does determine her peculiar contribution to human society . . . This is why women feel called to the spiritual motherhood of the cure of souls. Women should be priests just because priesthood is the most constructive and life giving function in the human society.' Dean Inge supported priesthood for women throughout the 1920s: 'I have assumed without argument that women will in the near future be admitted to ordination.' Lady Warrender advocated women's priesthood in 1924, and a Roman Catholic woman challenged the ban on women's priesthood in 1928. Whereas Canon Raven in 1928 approved the ordination of women, the bishop of Durham took a strong line against women's ordination. These views took rather the line of Raven and MacGee in 1919, and

> Church House was besieged . . . by enormous crowds eager to hear the debate on Women and the Priesthood arranged by the League of the Church Militant. Some time before the doors were opened a queue of people consisting mainly of women stretched half way down Great Smith Street and hundreds had to be turned away. . . . those who were lucky enough to get in spent a lively evening. The debate was presided over by the Master of the Temple.[43]

Women had obviously not achieved the central sacramental part of the clerical vocation by 1930; indeed women had not achieved full status in the homiletic and pastoral work of the Church by 1930. The fact is that women had gained but a small proportion of work within the Church; even by the 1980s much remained to be gained. Yet a beginning had been made and some work was being done by women which had been closed to them in the nineteenth century.

---

[43] *Challenge*, 8 Dec. 1916; Royden, *Women's Nature*, 1924; 'The Ministry of Women and the Tradition of the Church', *English Church Review*, Oct. 1916; Streeter and Picton-Turbervill, *Woman and the Church* (1917), p. viii; *Challenge*, 22 Apr. 1921, letter from Constance M. Coltman; *Evening Standard*, 1 Feb. 1921; Pamphlet, added Jan. 1930 in the Oberholzer Papers, File 63; CCR (1924), Lady Maud Warrender in a speech on the 'Social Life of the Village'; *Tablet*, 21 Apr. 1928; Raven, *Women and Holy Orders*; *Church Times*, 30 Mar. 1928; *Guardian*, 12 June 1919.

Index

Acland, Lady 12
Anglican Group for the Ordination of Women 134
Anglo-Catholic Congress (1930) 63
anti-feminism 5, 6
Aristotle 15
Armenia 61
A Talk about District Visiting 32
Austin, Sarah 9, 84
Australia 41

Baillie, Mrs E. 24
Balfour, A. J. 99
Barrett, Lady 121
Bedford, Bp. of 10
Benson, Abp. E. W. 95, 114
Bible Society 46
biblewomen's movement 46 ff., 53 ff.
Blunt, J. H. 10, 11, 20, 84
Blunt, Ven. R. F. L. 13
Booth, C. 5, 23, 27, 42, 54, 66, 71–2
Bridges, Revd C. 28
British Ladies Immigration Association 38
Burdett-Coutts, Baroness 14, 19, 21, 27
Burgon, Revd J. W. 7, 9, 66
Busk, Alice E. 87
Butler, Josephine E. 13–14

Cadman, Revd W. 29, 70
Calcutta, Bp. of 59
Campbell, Revd W. H. 36
Canada 41, 133
Canterbury Convocation 96 ff.
Carlile, Marie 56

Carlile, Preb. W. 55, 58
Carpenter, Mrs Boyd 21, 27, 37
Carter, Revd T. T. 63
'Cat and Mouse Act' 106
Cecil, Bp. G. 124
Cecil, Lord Hugh 100–1
Central Council/Committee for Women's Church Work 83, 92, 110, 118 ff., 123
Central Council of District Nursing 51
Champneys, Revd W. W. 70
Charity Organisation Society (COS) 33, 49, 54, 73
Chelmsford, diocese of 83
Cheltenham Ladies' College 89
China 60, 133
Christian Commonwealth 81, 121
Church Army 55 ff.
Church Assembly 24, 99
Church Congresses 95 ff.
  (1862) 53
  (1875) 63
  (1878) 8, 19, 20
  (1890) 13
  (1894) 40
  (1896) 25
  (1899) 98
  (1902) 18
  (1903) 101
  (1907) 57
  (1909) 81
  (1913) 16
  (1919) 88
Church League for Women's Suffrage (CLWS) 105–8, 111–12
church membership 5
Church Militant 87, 113, 129, 133
Church Missionary Society 59 ff.